FREE TRADE AND

ECONOMIC INTEGRATION

IN LATIN AMERICA

VICTOR L. URQUIDI

TRANSLATED FROM THE SPANISH BY MARJORY M. URQUIDI

FREE TRADE AND

ECONOMIC INTEGRATION

IN LATIN AMERICA

THE EVOLUTION OF

A COMMON MARKET POLICY

UNIVERSITY OF CALIFORNIA PRESS

BERKELEY AND LOS ANGELES, 1962

University of California Press
Berkeley and Los Angeles, California

Cambridge University Press
London, England

© *1962 by The Regents of the University of California*
Second Printing, 1962

Published with the assistance of a grant from the Ford Foundation

Library of Congress Catalog Card Number: 62-9167

Originally published in Spanish as *Trayectoria del Mercado Común
Latinoamericano* by Centro de Estudios Monetarios Latinoamericanos, México, 1960.

Designed by Frank J. Lieberman

Printed in the United States of America

PREFACE

THE PURPOSE OF THIS STUDY is to explain the recent
evolution of the concept of free trade in Latin America
and the manner in which it has been agreed to carry out
Latin American integration in general and the integration
of some groups of countries in particular.

The study is divided into three parts. Part I discusses
the effect of economic development on the composition
of Latin American imports, the nature of the small volume
of internal Latin American trade in the past, the early
steps taken toward trade and payments liberalization, and
the growing tendency to think of integration in terms of
industrial development. Part II gives an account of the
background of the various proposals for economic integration in the past few years, including their broad outlines and their translation into legal instruments, and the

measures taken up to the signature of the Montevideo Treaty establishing a free-trade area between seven Latin American countries. A chapter on the Central American experience and another on the proposals for payments compensation and for reciprocal credit are included. Part III reviews the present situation of the Latin American free-trade area and the problems it faces.

The studies of the Secretariat of the United Nations Economic Commission for Latin America have made such a fundamental contribution to the drawing up of governmental plans for intra-Latin American free trade and an ultimate common market that the author wishes to acknowledge their influence on the whole of the text that follows, rather than mention them with reference to every separate topic. At the end will be found a selected bibliography both of ECLA reports and of other articles and studies. A chronology of the Latin American common market and the text of the Montevideo Treaty appear as appendixes.

The author wishes to thank Mr. Javier Márquez, director of the Centro de Estudios Monetarios Latinoamericanos, for having given him the opportunity of writing this study and to acknowledge at the same time the valuable coöperation of the staff of the Centro with regard to documentation and bibliography.

V. L. U.

MEXICO CITY

TORRE LATINOAMERICANA,

MAY, 1960

THE SITUATION AND PROSPECTS of Latin American development have lately acquired new international significance. This is demonstrated by the Alliance for Progress proposed by the United States, by the greater participation of several European countries in the financing of Latin American development, and by the closer economic relations of Soviet-block countries with some countries in North and South America. Apart from these plans and trends, Latin America is becoming increasingly aware that the creation of a common market is essential to economic development. The movement toward Latin American economic integration is gaining momentum and attracting more attention from other parts of the world because of its intrinsic interest as well as its possible effect on international trade, especially trade with the United States, Western Europe, and Japan. The growth of trade in the European Economic Community, the formation of the European Free-Trade Association, and the discussion of similar proposals in Asia and Africa emphasize the importance of understanding the background and the main features of the present Latin American free-trade area, which with time may evolve into a common market of far-reaching consequences.

Events have moved so rapidly that it has been necessary to prepare for this edition a brief postscript to chapter 8 in order to discuss some of the more recent developments, such as the entry into force on June 1, 1961, of the Montevideo Treaty. This pact created the Latin American Free-Trade Association, composed of Argentina, Brazil, Chile, Mexico, Paraguay, Peru, and Uruguay, with Colombia and Ecuador as likely additional members. Chapter 7, on Central America, has also been brought up to date. Although it would not be possible to take into account all new events and the expanding bibliography on the problems of liberalizing intra-Latin American trade, the more significant items have been added to Appendix A and the bibliography.

The author trusts that English-language readers will find this exposition of an aspect of modern Latin American life useful and wishes to thank the University of California Press for publishing this translation, as well as Dr. John P. Harrison, of the Rockefeller Foundation, and Dr. William Diebold, Jr., of the Council on Foreign Relations, for having suggested it. He also wishes to thank his wife for having given the English text a clarity that it may have lacked in Spanish.

V. L. U.
Mexico City
July, 1961

CONTENTS

PART THREE

THE CURRENT SITUATION

APPENDIXES

TABLES

PART ONE

EVOLUTION OF

THE CONCEPT OF FREE TRADE

IN LATIN AMERICA

CHAPTER 1

THE CHANGING PATTERN OF

LATIN AMERICAN ECONOMIC

DEVELOPMENT

SINCE THE END of the Second World War, the Latin American economy has changed considerably. The outstanding structural feature has been the process of industrialization. In some countries this process has gone further than in others and has also started from a more advanced level; but it is present in all countries. Intensified industrial growth is now in the foreground of Latin America's economic policy —without interfering with the objectives pursued in other branches of activity or disturbing the balanced relationship that is advisable between different elements of the economic structure and between domestic and export development.

This new qualitative aspect in the growth of twenty republics with a total population of nearly 200 million is of special significance to their economic relations with the rest of the world; for it has an appreciable effect on the composition of their imports. Traditionally, in the early stages of industrialization, equipment and raw materials must be imported from foreign countries in which capital intensity is higher; but in due course, when export proceeds are insufficient to meet all import needs, the industrializing countries—as has been true of Latin America—are obliged to enter into more complex phases of self-supply in some kinds of equipment and intermediate products, as well as to provide as far as possible their own raw materials, in order to be able to continue importing heavier machinery, equipment, and other indispensable articles from the rest of the world. Imports of light consumer goods already have been largely replaced by domestic production, and this process is likely to go on.

Such a shift in the demand for imports not only affects trade with traditional supplying countries, but also influences the size and structure of trade between the Latin American countries themselves. Therefore, it is of interest to consider briefly how the composition of Latin American imports has changed under the impact of industrialization.

According to estimates made by the Secretariat of the United Nations Economic Commission for Latin America, the rate of increase in Latin America's gross national product was approximately 5.2 per cent annually during 1945–1955. In the same period, in spite of a population growth of 26 per cent, the total increase in *per capita* gross national product was 31 per cent and consumption increased by 40 per cent. This was not true to the same extent in all countries. In some, the *per capita* gross product increased considerably, in others it remained almost stationary. The latter group of countries includes Argentina, Bolivia, Chile, Uruguay, and Paraguay, all of which at present contribute less than a third of the gross product of Latin America. The center of gravity of economic activity has moved northward.

The rapid over-all expansion of the Latin American

economy was due in large measure to favorable conditions in world demand during the major part of the period under discussion, as reflected in an annual export gain of 5.4 per cent in real terms. The principal factor of improvement was, however, the price relationship between exports and imports, since the volume of exports increased only by 2.3 per cent a year.

In any event, the stimulus from abroad facilitated an increase in domestic investment and contributed to internal market conditions that were a powerful incentive to industrial development. As a result of restricted foreign-exchange resources and of deliberate promotion measures, industrial development began to substitute domestic output for imports competing with new national industries. On the other hand, in some cases, dependence on imports became greater because of the lack of timely government policies regarding local production of intermediate products and essential raw materials, including fuel. This was true even of agricultural and livestock products, for which sufficient resources and manpower were available.

The rising importance of income originating in industrial activity in Latin America becomes evident if it is considered that total product went up by 38 per cent between 1948 and 1955, but the industrial product 45 per cent. Between 1955 and 1958 the corresponding figures were 12 and 15 per cent. (See table 1.) Manufacturing industry at present accounts for about 20 per cent of the aggregate gross product and employs about 15 per cent of the labor force.

The composition of Latin American imports has shifted with the change in the structure of domestic production and under the influence of accompanying phenomena such as the relative growth of urban population and the consequent demand for manufactured consumer goods. To satisfy this market, domestic manufacturing industry has required expanded imports of raw materials and

TABLE 1. *Growth of Gross Product and Some of Its Components, Latin America: 1948–1958 (Index numbers, 1950 prices)*

					Increase in per cent	
	1948	1950	1955	1958	1948–1955	1955–1958
Gross domestic product	91	100	126	141	38	12
Manufacturing	90	100	131	151	45	15
Agriculture and livestock	96	100	122	132	27	8
Mining and petroleum	90	100	136	160	51	18
Construction	87	100	115	130	32	13
Trade and finance	93	100	126	142	35	13
Transport and communications	89	100	139	154	56	11
Government	89	100	119	126	34	6
Other services	89	100	120	143	35	19

SOURCE: ECLA, *Economic Bulletin for Latin America*, Vol. III, No. 2, and Vol. V, No. 2.

intermediate products, almost always at the expense of imports of finished consumer goods.

Between 1948 and 1955, the latter decreased from 25 to 23 per cent of the total, and raw materials and intermediate products rose from 29 to 34 per cent. At the same time, the percentage of fuel imports rose from 7 to 10. (See table 2.) The same relationships continued through 1958. The changes are more clearly appreciated by observing the increases in each class of imports, especially between 1950 and 1955 (in order to omit the still abnormal imports of capital goods in 1948). While imports of consumer goods, mainly durable, rose only 8 per cent during that five-year period, imports of raw materials and intermediate products went up 22 per cent and fuel imports 55 per cent. (See table 3.) Capital goods, which represent a third of the total, showed an increase of 16 per cent; under that heading

TABLE 2. *Composition of Latin American Imports, 1948–1958*
(*Per cent of total*)

Type of goods	1948	1950	1955	1958
Consumer goods	25	25	23	24
Fuels	7	8	10	10
Raw materials and intermediate products	29	33	34	33
Capital goods	39	34	33	33
Consumer goods and their materials[a]	54	59	60	59
Capital goods and their materials[b]	46	41	40	41
Finished goods[c]	57	53	50	52
Materials[d]	43	47	50	48

[a] Includes durable and nondurable consumer goods, fuels, and nonmetallic raw materials and intermediate products.

[b] Capital goods, plus metallic raw materials and intermediate products.

[c] Durable and nondurable consumer goods, and machinery and equipment for agriculture, industry, and transportation.

[d] Fuels, raw materials and intermediate products, and construction materials.

SOURCE: See table 3.

imports of industrial machinery and equipment rose 22 per cent and those of transport machinery and equipment 25 per cent. Between 1956 and 1958, all general categories rose about 13 per cent, but some of their components were more dynamic than others. For example, imports of nondurable consumer goods rose only 4 per cent, but durable goods 13 per cent; primary and intermediate metal products increased 17 per cent, nonmetal products only 9 per cent; and under capital goods, those intended for transport went up 30 per cent and those used in industry 17 per cent; in contrast, imports of machinery and equipment for agriculture and for construction went down.

Aggregate figures for Latin America naturally do not show many significant differences arising from the diverse

TABLE 3. *Composition of Latin American Imports, 1948–1958 (Millions of dollars, at 1955 prices)*

Type of goods	1948	1950	1955	1958	Increase in per cent		
					1948–1955	1950–1955	1955–1958
Consumer goods	1 498	1 426	1 541	1 708	3	8	11
Nondurable	*995*	*1 022*	*1 076*	*1 124*	8	5	4
Durable	*503*	*404*	*465*	*584*	−8	15	13
Fuels	498	508	787	853	58	55	8
Raw materials and intermediate products	1 995	2 098	2 568	2 852	29	22	11
Metal	*462*	*453*	*552*	*648*	19	22	17
Nonmetal	*1 533*	*1 645*	*2 016*	*2 204*	32	23	9
Capital goods	2 686	2 158	2 499	2 839	−7	16	14
Construction materials	*442*	*390*	*410*	*392*	−7	5	−4
Machinery and equipment for agriculture	*222*	*292*	*271*	*249*	22	−7	−8
Machinery and equipment for industry	*1 355*	*1 049*	*1 284*	*1 502*	−5	22	17
Machinery and equipment for transportation	*667*	*427*	*534*	*696*	−20	25	30
TOTAL[a]	6 814	6 355	7 535	8 520	11	19	13

[a] Includes a small amount of unclassified imports (from 2 to 3 per cent of the total).

SOURCE: ECLA, *Economic Bulletin for Latin America*, Vol. IV, No. 2, table 34,

economic structures of the countries. Moreover, the pattern of each country is influenced by its over-all import trend. In general, countries achieved a more favorable composition of their import trade if exports permitted them to raise their imports and to continue unrestricted purchases of essential goods and materials.

Another way of looking at the import structure is to group on one side consumer goods and their constituent materials and on the other side capital goods with their materials and parts. For Latin America as a whole, the former made up 59 per cent and the latter 41 per cent of the total during 1950–1958. It is interesting to note the differences by countries. In Argentina, Brazil, Colombia, and Peru, the percentage of capital goods and materials was generally more than 45; in both Mexico and Venezuela, it averaged about 50 (although not for the same reasons). In Cuba and Uruguay, which are less industrialized, it was 25 to 30; in the rest of the countries the ratio of capital goods and materials rose from 26 per cent to 39 per cent. In Chile, it was 43 per cent in 1950 and decreased (abnormally) to 18 per cent in 1958. (See table 4.)

Latin American countries undergoing industrialization have shown a tendency to increase their imports of primary or semiprocessed products (either for consumption or investment) more rapidly than those of finished goods. This reflects partly the replacement of imports through increased manufacturing capacity and, at the same time, the dependence of an expanding industry on essential supplies of intermediate products. It also foreshadows which sectors may be susceptible to replacement in the future. Moreover, it is an indication of the impact that industrial growth may have on less-developed countries in Latin America. Primary and semiprocessed products represented 48 per cent of all Latin American imports in 1958, but the percentage was higher in the more industrialized countries: For example,

TABLE 4. *Composition of Imports in Principal Latin American Countries, 1950 and 1958 (Per cent of total)*

Country	Consumer goods and their materials		Capital goods and their materials		Finished goods		Materials	
	1950	1958	1950	1958	1950	1958	1950	1958
All Latin America	59	59	41	41	53	52	47	48
Argentina	56	65	44	35	33	30	67	70
Brazil	51	56	49	44	52	45	48	55
Colombia	55	54	45	46	56	50	44	50
Cuba	83	70	17	30	67	64	33	36
Chile	57	82	43	18	43	54	57	46
Mexico	50	51	50	49	49	47	51	53
Peru	54	59	46	41	64	61	36	39
Uruguay	62	75	38	25	49	28	51	72
Venezuela	57	48	43	52	72	70	28	30
Other countries[a]	74	61	26	39	63	61	37	39

[a] In 1950, 9 per cent of total imports; in 1958, 12 per cent.
SOURCE: ECLA, *Economic Bulletin for Latin America*, Vol. IV, No. 2, tables 29 to 34. See footnotes to table 2 in this chapter.

in Brazil, Colombia, Chile, and Mexico it was approximately 50 to 55 per cent, and less than this in 1950, with the exception of Chile. On the other hand, in Cuba, Peru, Venezuela, and the rest of the countries, they made up only 30 to 40 per cent of the total, although this percentage tended to rise. Argentina and Uruguay are special cases because they had radically restricted their total imports so that by 1958 imports of raw materials accounted for 70 per cent.

These aggregates include some variants among their component parts which are worthwhile pointing out. For instance, the tendency to substitute imports of raw materials for finished goods has been more noticeable in consumer goods than in capital goods. As for finished goods, some countries have increased their imports of durable consumer goods and refined fuels more rapidly than their imports of other finished articles; other countries, especially the less developed, have accelerated their import rate of processed foodstuffs. But even though imports of finished capital goods have risen proportionately less, the growth of imports of transport and industrial equipment has been considerable—more so than in agricultural equipment.

Finally, among primary and semifinished products, imports of crude oil, of materials for the manufacture of consumer goods and, in some countries, of construction materials have increased.[1]

In spite of the mentioned effect of industrialization on imports in general, its impact on internal Latin American trade has barely begun to be felt. Until now, the expanding demand of Latin American manufacturing industry for raw materials and intermediate products has been met mainly by the traditional supplying countries. Nevertheless, without diminishing total imports from abroad, Latin America could increasingly use its rising productive capacity to provide part of its own additional needs.

In other words, the problem of replacement of imports should not be considered by each country in terms of its purely national interests but should be visualized within the broader and more flexible framework of the common interests of all Latin American countries. It has been estimated by the ECLA Secretariat that within fifteen years the value of intra-Latin American trade, which at present averages about 800 million dollars, could reach ten times that amount; and the trade pattern itself would be completely modified provided that this were made possible by coöperation among the more industrialized countries of Latin America.

---

[1] With regard to this and the preceding paragraph, see the analysis for the period 1948–1950 to 1954–1955 in ECLA's *Economic Survey of Latin America, 1956*, appendix on "Effects of postwar industrialization on the composition of imports."

CHAPTER 2

PRESENT INTRA-

LATIN AMERICAN TRADE

UP TO NOW, the replacement of imports has been conceived of as a strictly national phenomenon in each country; and intraregional trade has been more the expression of a natural complementarity, of geographic proximity, and of isolated and sporadic efforts to sell occasional surpluses of industrial or agricultural production. In the region as a whole, no systematic exchange of goods has existed among the Latin American republics.

Latin American imports from countries within the region have varied from 10 to 12 per cent of aggregate imports, with a total value of approximately 750 to 850 million dollars in recent years. (See table 5.) Nevertheless, 80 to 90 per cent of that trade has been conducted by seven southern countries—Argentina, Brazil, Chile, Peru, Uru-

TABLE 5. *Latin American Imports Originating in Latin America, 1946–1951 to 1958*

Imports	1946–1951 average	1953	1955	1958
Total (millions of dollars)	5 755	6 540	7 555	8 436
Those originating in Latin America (millions of dollars)	645	786	859	852
Per cent of total	11	12	11	10
Distribution (in per cent) by country of destination				
Argentina	28	27	29	32
Brazil	21	38	34	29
Chile	11	8	11	6
Peru	4	2	3	3
Uruguay	9	7	7	6
Bolivia	5	3	2	1
Paraguay	2	1	1	1
TOTAL (SEVEN COUNTRIES)	80	86	87	78
Colombia	4	3	3	2
Venezuela	5	2	1	2
Cuba	3	2	3	10
Mexico	2	—	—	1
Others[a]	6	7	6	7
TOTAL REMAINING COUNTRIES	20	14	13	22

[a] In 1946–1951, 7 per cent of total imports originating in Latin America; in 1953 and 1955, 10 per cent; and in 1958, 11 per cent.

SOURCE: 1946–1951 and 1954: ECLA, *Study of Inter-Latin American Trade*, table 11; 1955 and 1958, United Nations, *Direction of International Trade* (Statistical Papers, Series T, Vol. X, No. 8). Imports valued c.i.f.

guay, Bolivia, and Paraguay. In fact, the first two countries have participated to the extent of 49 per cent of the total in 1946–1951 and of more than 60 per cent in 1955 and 1958. The share of other countries in intra-Latin American imports is very small; for example, Colombia has accounted for 2 to 3 per cent, Venezuela for 1 to 2 per cent, Mexico for 1 per cent or less, Cuba for 3 per cent in 1955 and an exceptional 10 per cent in 1958, and the rest of the countries together for 5 to 6 per cent. (See table 5.)

However, some countries purchase a considerable share of their total imports from Latin America, notably Argentina, Brazil, Chile, and Uruguay, where it has varied from 20 to 30 per cent in different years. In Bolivia and Paraguay, the share has been at times substantially higher, reaching 36 to 46 per cent, although with considerable fluctuation from year to year. In almost all these countries, the share has been diminishing, which is not surprising in the light of the growing demand for imports of industrial products and machinery. At a lower level are Ecuador, El Salvador, Honduras, Peru, and, recently, Cuba, which import from Latin America from 7 to 15 per cent of their total purchases. In the other countries, except for Mexico and Venezuela, which obtain only 1 to 2 per cent of their imports from Latin America, the share varies from about 3 to 8 per cent. (See table 6.)

As for exports, Argentina, Brazil, and Venezuela have generally supplied more than 60 per cent of intra-Latin American imports, and in 1958 almost 80 per cent; Chile and Peru together have supplied 8 to 18 per cent; other countries have had little importance as suppliers—for example, Mexico, Uruguay, Paraguay, and Cuba account for only 2 to 3 per cent each and Colombia and Ecuador for 1 per cent each. (See table 7.)

It is thus evident that, broadly speaking, internal Latin American trade has been largely concentrated in some countries and that for only a few of these has it had any significance as export trade.

Apart from structural causes, the reason for this was that, until very recently, intra-Latin American trade has been conducted largely under bilateral agreements. The ab-

TABLE 6. *Ratio of Latin American Imports Originating in Latin America to Total Imports, by Importing Countries, 1946–1951 to 1958 (In per cent)*

Country	1946–1951 average	1953	1955	1958
Argentina	16	28	21	22
Brazil	12	23	22	18
Chile	27	20	24	13
Peru	14	6	9	7
Uruguay	26	28	27	36
Bolivia	38	36	28	17
Paraguay	43	25	46	25
Colombia	7	5	4	5
Venezuela	5	2	1	1
Ecuador	9	9	8	6
Cuba	4	3	4	10
Mexico	2	—	—	1
El Salvador	13	13	12	14
Honduras	12	7	7	10
Others[a]	8	4	..	..

[a] In 1946–1951, 5 per cent of total imports originating in Latin America; in 1953, 7 per cent.

SOURCE: 1946–1951 and 1953, ECLA, *Study of Inter-Latin American Trade*, table 10; 1955 and 1958, International Monetary Fund, *International Financial Statistics*, March 1960, pp. 28–29.

sence of these agreements among a group of countries has often made it difficult to increase trade. In 1955, an estimated 66 per cent of trade was transacted through bilateral accounts; if petroleum is omitted, 87 per cent. Nonetheless, the agreements had the result of both limiting and distorting trade. As will be seen below, in 1957 trade liberalization began with an attack on precisely the obstacles that prevented multilateral payments compensation and partial convertibility of balances.

But it is necessary to examine the precise nature of

TABLE 7. *Origin of Latin American Imports from Latin America,
1946–1951 to 1958 (In per cent)*

Exporting country	1946–1951 average	1953	1955	1958
Argentina	31	36	27	17
Brazil	24	16	19	20
Venezuela	7	18	21	40
Chile	8	10	8	5
Peru	10	6	6	3
Uruguay	3	2	4	2
Bolivia	—	—	1	—
Paraguay	2	1	3	2
Colombia	1	1	—	1
Ecuador	2	1	2	1
Cuba	3	3	2	2
Mexico	5	2	3	3
Others	4	4	4	4

SOURCES: same as for table 5.

intra-Latin American trade of recent years, in order to
appreciate its limitations. Until 1955, 45 to 55 per cent of
this trade was composed of food products, principally wheat
and wheat flour, coffee, and fresh fruit (bananas). Between
20 and 25 per cent consisted of fuels, mainly crude petroleum and to a lesser extent diesel oil, fuel oil, and gasoline.
Other raw materials made up 17 to 20 per cent of the trade,
especially agricultural products such as raw cotton, forestry
products (unprocessed and semiprocessed lumber), and, to
a lesser degree, metals and minerals including electrolytic
copper, lead, steel, and nitrate. (See table 8.)

Manufactured industrial products accounted for barely
3 per cent of total internal Latin American trade. The most
important of these were copper wire, cotton textiles, drugs
and medicines, and, in some years, rayon and woolen textiles. Although complete data are not available, trade in

TABLE 8. *Latin American Exports to Latin American Countries, by Principal Commodities, 1946–1951, 1953, and 1955 (In per cent)*

Commodity	1946–1951 average	1953	1955
Foodstuffs	48	52	45
Wheat	*15*	*21*	*17*
Coffee	*4*	*7*	*6*
Sugar	*8*	*5*	*5*
Fresh fruit (bananas, etc.)	*4*	*5*	*5*
Cattle	*4*	*2*	*1*
Other	*13*	*12*	*11*
Agricultural raw materials	14	13	17
Rough and partly worked timber	*8*	*6*	*10*
Cotton	*3*	*4*	*5*
Other	*3*	*3*	*2*
Mineral raw materials	5	6	4
Copper	*2*	*1*	*1*
Iron and steel	—	*3*	*1*
Lead	*2*	*1*	*1*
Nitrates	*1*	*1*	*1*
Other	—	—	—
Fuels	11	21	25
Crude petroleum	*4*	*8*	*13*
Fuel oil	*2*	*3*	*3*
Diesel oil	*1*	*3*	*4*
Gasoline	*3*	*7*	*3*
Other products	*1*	—	*2*
Manufactured goods	8	3	3
Copper wire	—	*1*	*1*
Cotton textiles	*5*	*1*	*1*
Pharmaceutical products	*1*	—	—
Other	*2*	*1*	*1*

SOURCE: ECLA, *Inter-Latin American Trade: current problems,* table 33.

manufactures probably has increased considerably since 1956, above all in steel products, paper, synthetic fertilizers, and electrical articles; and the export of vehicles and other durable goods has been initiated.

Manufactured goods and semiprocessed raw materials have encountered the most serious obstacles in trade among the Latin American countries. Part of these difficulties can be explained in terms of deficient transportation, both by sea and overland. However, another basic factor has been the stage of development of many Latin American industries which are still insufficiently consolidated and integrated; they have been afflicted by high unit costs and various kinds of hindrances. In some countries, acute inflation, besides affecting the costs of certain processes, has made it more difficult to establish regular and firmly based export relations. The incidence of multiple exchange-rate systems, and on occasion the extreme shortage of foreign exchange, have also contributed to raising costs. On the other hand, the lack of medium and long-term credit required by more complex manufactures and the inefficient operation of some of the bilateral compensation agreements have had similar effects. Many countries have imported manufactures and materials from outside Latin America without realizing that sources of supply could have been developed within the region. Another trade problem has been the absence of standardized specifications, for example, in iron and steel. As is evident, there are many factors and some of them are related not only to internal Latin American trade, but to the expansion of national markets.

The trade policy of the Latin American countries, outside of payments agreements and some partial attempts at integration, has not been particularly directed toward favoring regional trade. Although agriculture is subject to regulation in most countries, little effort has been made to promote long-term economic complementarity. Moreover, many shortages in foodstuffs and other agricultural and livestock products have been met by imports from outside Latin America; this may have been due to reasons of transport or of price, to special problems of financing, or other factors. During 1955–1957, Latin American countries did a reciprocal trade of 303 million dollars in foodstuffs, and imported 410 million dollars worth from the rest of the world; most of these foods—wheat, flour, cooking oils and fats, dairy products, rice, livestock and meat, fruit—are commodities which Latin America also exports.

It has been the same with other primary and intermediate products, such as metals and fuels. Latin American countries purchase from their own region only 10 per cent of their crude and refined petroleum import requirements, less than 10 per cent of their imports of lead and zinc, and about 25 per cent of their imports of copper ingots and semiprocessed copper, although they are, as a whole, net exporters of all these commodities.

Even within the patterns imposed by present custom tariffs, trade treaties, and the General Agreement on Tariffs and Trade (GATT), a greater effort could probably have been made to promote intra-Latin American trade, above all by the countries not shackled by exchange restrictions.

CHAPTER 3

FROM TRADE LIBERALIZATION

TO COÖRDINATED ECONOMIC

DEVELOPMENT

EARLIER ATTEMPTS

THE INTEGRATION OR union of several countries is not a new concept in Latin America. After the various countries achieved independence, attempts were made in this direction, although mainly politically motivated. Projected or accomplished federations in Central America, in Greater Colombia, and between Bolivia and Peru, as well as other proposals and treaties, had few economic implications. Before and at the beginning of the Second World War, various Pan American and other conferences took under consideration the possibility of the economic integration of the whole of Latin America or of groups of countries, but no definite plans were worked out. Some of these proposals gave attention in a general way to the resultant economic benefits, but others went further, such as the proposals made in 1941 to create a River Plate Customs Union which would be extended to bordering countries. In 1939, Argentina and Brazil already had planned a complementation and free-trade agreement with respect to new industrial activities. Although none of these arrangements were carried out, they served as precedents for later economic integration proposals.[1]

During the Second World War, coöperation among the Latin American countries and between these and the United States was closer, and not only for economic but for strategic reasons. It was suggested that, among other possibilities, Latin America might form an "economic bloc" either as a region or with the rest of the Western Hemisphere.[2] "Regional" integration plans were also proposed or drafted in other parts of the world, notably in Europe. The concept of economic coöperation among countries of similar levels of development gained considerable strength. It was evident that the postwar period would bring into being a whole new constellation of power in the world and that the weaker countries, whatever the degree of their participation in the armed conflict, would be at a disadvantage if they did not unite their forces.

Nevertheless, during and after the war only scattered attempts were made in Latin America to establish more effective arrangements for regional coöperation, especially in trade and payments. Argentina signed treaties of this

---

[1] Regarding these and later proposals, see ECLA, *Study of inter-Latin American Trade and its prospects: southern zone of Latin America* (United Nations, 1954), chapter iii.

[2] A valuable discussion of several of these ideas and proposals is to be found in Javier Márquez, *Posibilidad de bloques económicos en América Latina* (México, El Colegio de México, Jornadas 16, 1944), chapters iii–v.

type with Chile, Paraguay, Bolivia, Peru, and other countries, which were intended to solve payments problems and
remove obstacles from the traditional flows of trade. Given
the very low tariff levels, the elimination of exchange restrictions frequently was equivalent to liberation of trade.
But these agreements were not firmly grounded nor did they
attempt, in general, to advance systematically toward a more
profound economic integration.

In Central America, following its history of recurrent
federalist proposals, the postwar period brought negotiations
or revisions in some of the bilateral free-trade treaties, especially between El Salvador and its neighbors. The essential
element of these trade agreements was the concept of integration based on potential complementarity and on the consideration of population problems and the need for joint
development of the Central American region. The countries
of Greater Colombia—Ecuador, Colombia, and Venezuela
—also tried in 1948 to revive the idea of a customs union
among themselves, but without success.

However, as already noted, most internal Latin American trade has always been carrried out between the southern countries of South America; and after the war this trade
was gravely hampered by a series of import barriers and,
particularly, by the extraordinary complications of the
exchange-control systems that these countries had been
obliged to adopt to offset deteriorating external conditions.
It was natural then that in practice this situation should
prove to be a strong incentive to the search for basic solutions in favor of freer trade among the countries of Latin
America.

TOWARD PAYMENTS TRANSFERABILITY

THERE HAS ALWAYS been a desire to simplify exchange restrictions and to facilitate transfers of balances of bilateral payments agreements. But during the postwar period, the balance-of-payments problem proved to be too great for the limited possibilities and inelastic policies of the International Monetary Fund. Therefore, various other partial solutions were considered. In Europe, the influence of the Monetary Fund was even diminished because of the trade-liberation programs and the accompanying foreign-exchange-transferability arrangements through the European Payments Union.

Latin America, momentarily provided with exceptional foreign-exchange reserves (although not all freely convertible) at the end of the war, had no payments problem to compare with the European in character or magnitude. Nonetheless, with postwar readjustment, the fundamental trends of the balances of payments became evident. It was felt advisable to establish some mechanism of payments transfers which would at least permit an increase in the volume of intraregional trade, and which would also be aimed at multilateralizing the use of bilateral balances of European currencies, since trade was being resumed with Europe where inconvertibility prevailed. For this purpose, ECLA was asked during its first session in June, 1948, to study "the practicability and desirability of establishing, at the earliest possible opportunity, as a transitional measure, machinery for the multilateral compensation of international payments among the countries of Latin America, as well as between them and the countries of the rest of the world."

A report on the problem was requested from the staff of the International Monetary Fund, and consideration was also to be given to specific proposals of the Uruguayan government, as well as to other ideas.[3] Although presented to ECLA in 1949,[4] the report never led to any definite action both because its conclusions were not very positive and because the dollar shortage began to ease a year later. The authors of the report examined the payments problems of Latin America in order to study the possibilities of multilateral compensation of Latin American currencies and of dollar savings in trade and payments between the region and Europe. They found that the payments difficulties were in general not caused by lack of an adequate technical mechanism for compensation, but by the fact that "the situation is actually one of payments deficit which cannot be corrected by technical devices." As for the practical possibility of multilateral compensation within Latin America, they concluded that the ratio of bilateral to total foreign trade was too low, that credit balances that could be settled multilaterally were not more than 10 to 15 per cent of all balances, and that "the step from bilateral to multilateral clearing within a small group is unlikely to be directly very effective in increasing the volume of trade." They judged that it would not be useful to a group of moderately complementary countries unless 70 to 80 per cent of their balances could be compensated.

---

[3] An agreement for the creation of an Inter-American Bank, based on a Mexican proposal and signed by eight Latin American countries and the United States in 1940, included the possibility that the bank would act as a "clearing house" and "would facilitate by all possible means the transfer of international payments." See Eduardo Villaseñor, "El Banco Interamericano," *Ensayos Interamericanos*, Mexico, 1944, p. 85. See also, by the same author, "The Inter-American Bank: Prospects and Dangers," *Foreign Affairs*, Vol. 20, No. 1, October, 1941.

[4] ECLA, *Multilateral Compensation of International Payments in Latin America*, Doc. E/CN.12/87, May 27, 1949.

337.9 Ur6
c./

The actual situation was that about half of the intra-regional trade in Latin America was bilaterally financed. Argentina was a creditor of all Latin American countries with which it had bilateral agreements, except Brazil, and the latter was a constant creditor of Chile. At the same time, Argentina and Brazil had credit balances of several European currencies. These balances were gradually reduced in 1948 and 1949 through imports of European products and partial settlement in dollars. The pound sterling had begun to be transferable in Europe and in Latin America. Paraguay was permitted to use sterling balances to cover its bilateral debts to Argentina and Brazil. But the Monetary Fund did not find sufficient elements to ensure the success of a general system of multilateral compensation, either among the Latin American countries or between these and Europe.

The authors pointed out many other obstacles, such as the paucity of statistical information, discrepancies in methods of valuation as well as in the scope of the agreements, the probable reluctance of the northern countries to participate in any system which did not provide freely convertible balances, the administrative complications, the multiplicity of exchange rates, "the disposition of the foreign exchange proceeds of foreign-owned export companies," and the lack of a tradition of close coöperation between central banks. The results were "difficult to forecast" and the effort would be out of proportion to the benefits to be received. "For the immediate future," the report reads, "perhaps the most promising approach is an exploration of the possibilities of triangular offsets and of some further use of sterling."

As for trade with Europe, it was also recommended that existing agreements be improved, that triangular compensations be attempted, and that the pound sterling be more generally used, especially by the countries to the south. The report gave several examples of possible triangular compensation among Latin American countries and also between two of the latter and one European country.

During the same ECLA session which discussed the Monetary Fund report, the Uruguayan delegation recommended the establishment of an "Inter-American organization for economic coöperation," the essence of which would be a regional mechanism for payments compensation. But the Commission, in plenary session, considering conditions to be still unfavorable to such a proposal, only agreed to take note of the conclusions drawn by the Fund report and to recommend that the executive secretary request the latter agency to make a new study, with the collaboration of "the appropriate international organizations," in order to explore "the possibility of arrangements for partial multilateral compensation of international payments among Latin American countries as well as between them and other countries" (resolution adopted on June 10, 1949).

Succeeding years saw an expansion of the system of bilateral payments or compensation agreements between various Latin American countries, mainly those in the south; and also between the southern countries—especially Argentina—and some farther to the north. Argentina, Brazil, Paraguay, and Uruguay tended to carry on their transactions with areas outside the dollar zone and with the rest of Latin America almost exclusively by bilateral agreements. But frequently measures of liberalization and simplification were taken in an attempt to introduce greater flexibility; on occasion, some multilateral transfers of balances, both in national currency like the Argentine, or in sterling, were permitted. At the same time, some progress was made in the partial settlement of balances through payments in convertible currency, and more realistic exchange rates were adopted for the accounts, just as there was also a decrease in the number of rates applicable to different transactions. Nonetheless, some of the reforms had negative effects on the volume of trade by eliminating high-cost items; and the continuation of bilateral agreements with their implications made it practically impossible to increase trade with Latin American countries having a freely convertible currency.[5]

The ECLA Secretariat continued exploring the possibility of multilateralizing payments. On the one hand, it examined the position of some Latin American currencies in their trade with Europe and the theoretical feasibility of associating Latin American countries, in a limited fashion, with the mechanism of the European Payments Union, so that those countries could transfer among themselves the balances they received through the Union. On the other hand, in its later meetings and with the coöperation of groups of experts, ECLA considered various ways of finding a multilateral solution to the internal Latin American problem.

As for the question of compensations with Europe, the Latin American representatives to the annual meeting of the International Monetary Fund, held in Paris in 1950, examined jointly and unofficially the possible repercussions of the European Payments Union on trade with Latin America. In the 1951 and 1952 sessions of ECLA this matter was again taken under consideration and was afterward analyzed by an ECLA consultant in a report which was presented to the fifth session of the Commission in 1953; in this report, on the basis of a survey of opinions within the European Payments Union itself, a study was made of various alternatives to the possible use of the Union mechanism for the transfer of European balances among Latin American countries.[6] It was made clear that notwithstanding the

---

[5] On the questions dealt with in this paragraph, see the following ECLA publications: *Study of inter-Latin American Trade* (United Nations, 1956), chapter v, and *Inter-Latin American Trade: current problems* (United Nations, 1957), pp. 21–48.

[6] ECLA, *Possibility of Effecting Multilateral Compensation Settlements between Latin American and European Countries through the European Payments Union*, a report by Robert Triffin, Doc. E/CN.12/299, March 4, 1953.

increasing degree of transferability among European currencies, with the consequent multilateral compensations, which even included overseas territories and other regions associated with those currencies, Latin America's relations with Europe had not benefited from this trend toward partial convertibility. Despite the advantages which would attend universal multilateralism, the general situation still did not permit it. Therefore, it was advisable at least to try to avoid purely bilateral compensations, and to expand the system through triangular and other settlements.

Even assuming that the International Monetary Fund could, through its own mechanisms, contribute to that type of partial multilateralization, interim measures were urgently needed. It was not enough for Latin American countries simply to enter the system of transferable sterling accounts, since several European countries still did not accept balances in that currency. However, Latin American participation in the compensations of the European Payments Union could yield certain benefits, even though limited. The author felt that the conclusion of a Latin American Payments Union would not be practicable "and would be of little value in itself in view of the scant trade relations now existing, or likely to develop, among the Latin American countries themselves"; nevertheless, "Latin American transferability might become far more important in connection with European settlements."

In brief, the specific proposal was that Latin American countries so desiring should participate only in the mechanism of compensation of the European Payments Union and not as full members with rights to credit and the consequent obligations. Even so, the procedure would have limitations since the European nations did not wish to acquire freely balances of Latin American currencies, transferable or not, and therefore they could only accept limited compensations which would not affect the over-all situation of each European country in the Union. In the final months of 1952, the Union experimented with a system of voluntary compensation, that is, nonautomatic, on the basis of information furnished by its members concerning their bilateral Latin American accounts, in order to estimate the extent of possible compensations. But the results proved to be modest.

The report also considered the possibility of a system of automatic compensations of the first category, namely, those which would not increase the balance of a European country with respect to a Latin American country in the Payments Union; and one of compensations of the second category, namely, those which could be restricted to the European countries and subject to the system of mutual guarantees of the Union. No practical result came from any of these proposals.

Nevertheless, in 1955 the so-called Hague Club was established, according to which Western Germany, the Netherlands, and the United Kingdom decided to coördinate their payments agreements with Brazil in such a way as to permit the balances to be settled in currencies of any of the first three countries. Later Austria, Belgium, France, Italy, and Luxemburg joined the arrangement. Thus Brazil was enabled to transfer with considerable freedom, except in the dollar area, its principal balances of European currencies. Argentina, in turn, negotiated in 1956 a similar arrangement with the same European countries, plus Switzerland and the Scandinavian countries, which was called the Paris Club.[7] But no compensations of balances were ever accomplished *between* Argentina and Brazil, that is, there was no communication between the two "clubs"; and although the advantages of this type of transaction and its extension to

---

[7] Cf. Robert Triffin, *Europe and the Money Muddle: From Bilateralism to Near-convertibility, 1947–1956* (New Haven, Yale University Press, 1957), p. 217.

other intra-Latin American payments were weighed on various occasions, it seems that no definite action was ever taken.[8]

To find multilateral solutions between Latin American countries, ECLA continued collecting information on intraregional trade and payments, and on ways to harmonize the functioning of different bilateral agreements, for instance, by means of a standard agreement, to be followed by a multilateral convention.[9] Special account was taken of problems arising from the continuation of the bilateral system, which blocked any attempt or program intended to broaden or diversify trade between Latin American countries. These ideas were discussed in successive sessions of ECLA between 1952 and 1955, and they resulted in the creation, in September, 1955, of the ECLA Trade Committee, which undertook the search for formulas of coöperation both with respect to payments and to the policy of liberalization of intraregional trade. This new stage in the progress toward Latin American economic integration will be discussed in chapter 4.

RECOGNITION OF THE BASIC INDUSTRIAL PROBLEMS

RECOGNITION OF the difficulties inherent in industrialization has given a special character to thinking about trade liberalization in Latin America. Latin American countries, some more than others, are engaged in programs or activities of industrial development in varying stages, from the simple

---

[8] In 1955, the Ibero-American Institute for Economic Coöperation, of Madrid, published the bases for a hypothetical payments union between Spain and ten Latin American countries. Nothing resulted from this scheme either.

[9] See the reports cited in footnote 5.

one of the processing of a raw material or a basic foodstuff for export purposes to the complex one of the manufacture of industrial machinery. In between is the entire range of manufactures, including consumer goods, iron and steel, chemical and pharmaceutical products, building materials, automobile parts, and household articles. As has already been stated, industrialization today cannot be separated from and, frequently, is an essential part of economic development.

It has often been found that domestic markets, even when growing, are insufficient to support manufacturing plants of the size needed for low unit costs, especially as regards basic industries. Nonetheless, Latin American countries have been willing to pay that price—high unit cost— for industrialization, being guided by a series of criteria, economic and otherwise, which are based on a more general consideration of the problem of development. In particular, rapid population expansion, intensified in the working-age sector, has made it imperative to absorb into industrial activities the excess labor created by advances in agricultural techniques or by rural emigration to the cities. Nationalistic attitudes toward natural resources and the deliberate development of these resources to benefit the nation have likewise been factors contributing to forms of industrial growth which would not have been encouraged by ordinary market forces.

But, perhaps more than anything else, the instability of exchange resources after the war, the sometimes uncontrollable demand for imports, and the relatively modest long-term foreign capital inflow, both public and private, were the elements which most conditioned the measures taken by Latin America to activate industrial development. It is normal that industrialization in a country that has not, by definition, attained modern economic structures and technologies should be confronted with innumerable internal obstacles and aggressive external competition. This process is made all the more difficult when balance-of-payments problems necessarily bring about systems of quantitative, tariff, and exchange restrictions under pressure of events and not as a result of a carefully thought-out plan. Behind the network of import-and-exchange controls are hidden distortions of the price-and-cost structure which, taken together with restricted supply, have not always led to an adequate industrial development nor to one fully justified by the domestic market.

Notwithstanding the unfavorable conditions prevailing in some countries and taking into account the more rational industrial development in others, the growth of manufacturing in Latin America has been rapid and has released exchange resources formerly spent on imports of consumer goods so that they may be used for machinery and equipment and for essential raw materials. As already seen by examination of the composition of imports, the proportion of consumer goods has been reduced, and this reduction indicates substitution of domestic production for imports. In some kinds of consumer goods, imports have been almost entirely replaced, especially in some of the more industrialized countries of Latin America, so that increases in consumption may be easily satisfied by means of established or projected productive capacity. There are even frequent examples of excess available capacity.

If the process of replacing industrial imports carries over to such basic industries as steel and chemical products and to the more advanced industries of precision machinery and the manufacture of durable goods and heavy machinery, the limitations of domestic markets become more evident. Technical units of operation in important phases of heavy industry, in addition to requiring large-scale investments, need a widespread market in order to be profitable. This has been the basis for industrialization in the United

States and other countries with high concentrations of productive equipment.

In Latin American countries, even those with relatively broader geographical and human resources, a combination of market, technology, and balance-of-payments factors accounts for a situation in which continued progress in industrialization is only possible if the level of purchasing power rises above that existing or anticipated within the boundaries of a single nation. It is not simply a question of attempting complementarity solutions between countries, with the resultant specialization; but rather of obtaining from the reciprocal action of additional markets a permanent new dimension which will economically justify larger scales of production, lower unit costs, and a fuller utilization of opportunities of production and consumption.

Since 1950 increasing attention has been given to the knowledge and comparison of the evolution of some basic industries of Latin America, and also to the numerous agricultural, fishery, and mining activities. A series of meetings, technical in nature and mainly held under the auspices of United Nations agencies, have been attended by representatives of interested Latin American countries and by specialists from all over the world. They have begun an objective examination of the present situation and of prospects and possibilities of industries such as iron and steel and their manufactures, pulp and paper, transport equipment including passenger automobiles, petroleum and derivatives, electric energy, and railroad cars; in addition, they have studied the more primary activities such as fisheries, livestock raising, and others. At the same time, they have given careful and continuous consideration to problems of land and sea transportation. The economic development, especially industrial, of the different Latin American countries has begun to be thought of as not only parallel but interdependent. This does not preclude, naturally, its continuing to be intimately linked to present and future events in the international markets for basic products.

Precisely this last prospect gives stronger impetus to Latin American integration and the common-market proposals. It is no longer assumed that Latin American trade can develop solely on the basis of products which are already being traded or products which in various countries only need to have a few artificial barriers lifted in order to be traded. With the participation of large private industrial groups and official agencies, there is a new idea of trade which conceives of products issuing from still nonexistent factories and industries now barely outlined, but sure to come into existence.

Even on the basis of relatively optimistic projections of Latin America's capacity to pay for imports and of the availability of foreign capital, the total amount of foreign-exchange receipts in 1975 is not expected to be sufficient to meet the demand for commodities which, unless there is an intensive effort to industrialize, will have to be imported in order to make possible a moderate increase in *per capita* product. According to ECLA's important study,[10] which outlines the respective projections, Latin America will be faced with the alternative of industrializing or condemning itself to a standstill or even a recession to lower living standards. And for the reasons already mentioned, the phase of industrialization which is beginning to develop will have to be conditioned by coöperation and trade. The most important internal Latin American trade of the future will be in industrial equipment and machinery, rather than in foodstuffs and raw materials.

The analysis and reasoning that leads the ECLA Secre-

---

[10] ECLA, "Influence of the Common Market in Latin American Economic Development," in *The Latin American Common Market* (United Nations, 1959).

tariat to these conclusions can be summed up in the following way:

The annual rate of increase in the *per capita* product of Latin America reached 2.7 per cent between 1945 and 1955, because of exceptional conditions in the demand for and the international prices of traditional export commodities. In the last five years the average increase in *per capita* product has been barely 1 per cent; so during the next fifteen years the rate of growth must recover from the loss it has suffered and be assured an average approximating that of the first ten postwar years. It is estimated that, given the probable population increase of 2.6 per cent a year, which will mean a total of 300 million inhabitants by 1975, the gross product will have to rise 5.4 per cent a year, a rate which by no means represents an exaggerated objective in the light of past experience and of what is achieved or projected in other parts of the world. But, according to the study made of the prospects for an increase in the demand for Latin American export commodities, and assuming as high a capital inflow from abroad as may be compatible with foreseeable payment obligations, Latin America would only be able to raise its purchasing power abroad by 3 per cent a year and still balance its international accounts. If this annual 3 per cent is to permit an average increase in product of 5.4 per cent, imports must be replaced on a massive scale.

The extent of replacement may be appreciated as a whole if it is borne in mind that the ratio of imports to gross Latin American product would have to be reduced from the 13 to 16 per cent on record between 1945 and 1955 to 10.5 per cent in 1970 and to 7.7 per cent in 1975. Even with a lower average rate of growth of product of 4.65 per cent a year, the import ratio would need to shrink to 8.9 per cent in 1975. In absolute terms, these figures mean that the foreseeable export trend together with a favorable assumption about the utilization of foreign capital, less amortization, dividends, and interest charges on the total foreign debt, would permit eventual imports totaling 11 billion dollars a year, in round numbers, during the five-year period between 1970 and 1975 (at 1950 prices). During 1954–1956, imports averaged 8 billion dollars. Exports would be expected to rise from 8.4 billion dollars in 1954–1956 to 13 billion in 1970 and to 15 billion in 1975. All of this is based on the assumption that by 1965 the inflow of foreign capital would be 2.7 billion (as against 1.1 billion a year in 1945–1956) and that by 1970 it would still amount to 2.3 billion; which would require amortization and service of 3.9 billion in 1970 and of 4.6 billion by 1975. (See table 9.)

The export projection was based on available studies of probable future demand, in the rest of the world, for

TABLE 9. *Projection of Available Latin American Import Resources* (*Millions of dollars at 1950 prices*)

Import resources	1954–1956 average	1965	1970	1975
Exports of goods and services	*8 429*	*11 294*	*13 109*	*15 276*
Loans and private capital from abroad	*1 081*	*2 700*	*2 271*	*325*
Service and amortization on loans and capital from abroad	*−1 294*	*−3 389*	*−3 933*	*−4 583*
Resources available for payment of imports and services	8 216	10 605	11 447	11 018

SOURCE: ECLA, "Influence of the Common Market on Latin American Economic Development," table 6, in *The Latin American Common Market.*

twelve foodstuffs, nine agricultural primary products, and seven mineral products. Account was taken of Latin American demand for the same products. Although exports to the United States, Canada, and western Europe, together representing the most important market, could increase between 49 and 83 per cent by 1975 (at 1954–1956 prices), those to other areas could expand between 262 and 422 per cent. Commodities most likely to undergo export growth are minerals (especially, iron ore, zinc, and copper) which are expected to increase by 106 to 163 per cent. It is estimated that foodstuffs and agricultural raw materials may rise to a considerably less extent, between 40 and 75 per cent, in particular oilseeds, fish and fish products, wool, wood, corn (maize), cacao, and coffee. Cotton, wheat, meat, sugar, and hides have very weak prospects for the next fifteen years.

The commodity projections taken as a whole also made possible a consideration of the extent to which different countries could share in the expansion of exports until 1975. While such an increase might reach 150 per cent for one country (Peru), around 100 per cent for five (Bolivia, Brazil, Chile, Mexico, and Venezuela) and 50 to 75 per cent for Colombia, Ecuador, Paraguay, and Central America, it will probably be only between 25 and 50 per cent for the rest (Argentina, Cuba, Uruguay); in the last three mentioned, the rise in exports will be less than the foreseeable gain in population.

The required replacement of imports is closely related to one of the fundamental assumptions of the cited projection of an annual 5.4 per cent increase in gross product. In order to achieve such a rate of general growth it would be necessary to increase aggregate fixed investment from its present ratio of 17.2 per cent of gross product to a minimum of 22.1 per cent in 1975, assuming, at the same time, that the average productivity of capital should rise about 13 per cent. Since 23 out of every 100 dollars of fixed gross investment represent the *c.i.f.* cost of imported machinery and equipment, it is estimated that by 1975 it will be necessary to import (at 1950 prices) 8.6 billion dollars' worth of industrial machinery in order to satisfy the demand implicit in the mentioned investment ratio, in comparison with the 2.2 billion dollars' worth that was imported in 1954–1956. Such future imports would be obviously impossible, for it has been seen that even under favorable assumptions, Latin America would only have available 11 billion dollars by 1975 for the payment of all of its imports, and of this amount 1.8 billions would be allocated for the purchase of basic products within Latin America itself. If 94 per cent of the exchange available for extraregional imports were used to import machinery, the remaining 6 per cent could not cover other vital needs. It is also essential that Latin America produce the greatest possible proportion of the machinery and equipment that it is going to require, together with their components and materials. The value of machinery imports would have to be limited to 3.7 billion dollars, and it is calculated that the region would need to increase its output of machinery 26 times by 1975, from 200 million dollars in 1954–1956 to 5.4 billions. This would have to be the cornerstone of Latin America's common economic development and, at the same time, one of the mainstays of future intraregional trade.

In the same way, by projecting the demand for the principal products and groups of products that will be required in Latin America for final and intermediate consumption, it must be concluded that regional supplies should be substituted as rapidly as possible for imports from abroad—especially when they are key items and a heightened demand is anticipated. This replacement—and the development effort it signifies—must be carried out for a great variety of agricultural, mining, and industrial products. A few examples will illustrate the enormous change that will have to take place and, at the same time, how this will affect trade between Latin American countries.

The possibility has already been mentioned of eventually eliminating almost completely extraregional imports of agricultural raw materials and foodstuffs. According to ECLA's estimates for 1975, Latin American consumption of milk and milk products, pork, and cotton fiber, will probably be two and a half to three times higher than in 1954–1956; its consumption of sugar, beef, cacao, and coffee will slightly more than double; and its consumption of wheat, rice, bananas, and mutton will almost double. With the exception of wheat and dairy produce, of which 8 per cent and 1.3 per cent of consumption will still have to be imported by 1975, the other commodities—including edible oils and fats—can be produced in Latin America. This assumes, of course, that improved agricultural techniques will make possible the volume of production needed to satisfy both Latin American and export demand. By achieving these goals, intraregional trade in agricultural commodities could triple by 1975.

The outlook is similar for the principal mining products. Latin American demand for copper should increase more than five times by 1975, but 80 per cent of this demand can be met by domestic production, with intraregional trade increasing more than fifty times. According to forecasts, the demand for fuels will quadruple, but only a minimum of what is needed will have to be imported from outside the region in 1975.

By multiplying its intraregional trade twelve times, Latin America could supply 86 per cent of its demand for steel and semimanufactured steel products, instead of the present 39 per cent; 32 million tons instead of 2.6 million. Unless it accomplishes this, Latin America will have to use 45 per cent of its available foreign exchange in 1975 for the importation of steel, which would be out of the question.

It is estimated that the demand for basic chemicals, of which 25 per cent is now met by 600 million dollars' worth of imports, might increase two and a half times. Latin American production of sodium products, petrochemical products, acids, plastics, synthetic fibers, and similar items should quadruple in order to reduce the import ratio, in which case trade within Latin America of these products might multiply by 140 times.

Most Latin American countries might reach self-sufficiency in paper and paperboard, of which 38 per cent is now imported from abroad. Consumption will have more than quadrupled by 1975 and it is expected that intraregional trade could increase more than a hundredfold.

The purchase of passenger cars has been limited in many Latin American countries by lack of foreign exchange. Only 115,000 vehicles were imported in 1954–1956, at a cost of 300 million dollars. By 1975 it is estimated that 1,800,000 new units a year will be required which, if imported from outside the region, would use up close to 4,500 million dollars, or 40 per cent of the foreign exchange available at that time. As in the case of machinery, steel, and other products, this would represent an impossible rise in imports. Latin American production, already begun in Argentina and Brazil and soon to be undertaken in Mexico, would have to satisfy at least 75 per cent of the yearly demand for automobiles, which would signify an intraregional trade of 540 million dollars by 1975.

All these projections aim at a final goal of an annual intraregional trade of more than 8 billion dollars, of which 32 per cent would be machinery and equipment, 37 per cent intermediate products (including fuels), 13 per cent agricultural commodities, 6.5 per cent passenger cars, and 11.5

per cent miscellaneous. (See table 10.) By contrast, in 1955, foodstuffs and other agricultural commodities represented 61 per cent, mineral products 4 per cent, fuels 25 per cent, and manufactured products 3 per cent.

TABLE 10. *Projection of Intra-Latin American Trade to 1975*

	Millions of dollars		Per cent of total	
Product	1954–1956	1975	1954–1956	1975
Machinery and equipment	—	2 671	—	32
Passenger automobiles	—	540	—	7
Steel and semimanufactured steel products	51	764	7	9
Copper and semimanufactured copper products	3	180	—	2
Fuels	196	879	26	11
Chemical products	8	1 125	1	13
Paper and board	—	130	—	2
Cotton yarn and textiles	8	360	1	4
Staple agricultural commodities	338	1 083	45	13
Other products	152	605	20	7
TOTAL	756	8 337	100	100

SOURCE: same as for table 9.

Table 11 summarizes the principal projections of demand by 1975 for the different products referred to as well as projections of regional supply. As the ECLA studies explicitly point out, these projections are not forecasts but only indications. Based on reasonable assumptions and on the examination of quantitative relationships in the past within the area and in other parts of the world, they give an idea of the magnitude of the problems confronting Latin America in its economic development and of the role to be played by intraregional trade. Here is the modern justification for

TABLE 11. *Projections of Latin American Demand and Regional Supply in 1975, for Principal Products or Groups of Products*

Products	1954–1956 average		1975		Increase in per cent	
	De-mand	Per cent of re-gional supply	De-mand	Per cent of re-gional supply	De-mand	Re-gional supply
Machinery and equipment (millions of dollars)	2 222	9	9 122	00	311	2 018
Passenger automobiles (thousands)	115	—	1 790	73	1 456	...
Steel and semimanufactured steel products (thousands of tons)	6 600	39	37 600	86	470	1 155
Copper and semimanufactured copper products (thousands of tons)	70	50	540	82	671	1 166
Petroleum and derivatives (millions of tons)	47	67	201	96	328	513
Chemical products (millions of dollars)	2 300	75	8 155	89	255	321
Paper and board (millions of dollars)	370	62	1 545	86	318	481
Cotton yarn and textiles (thousands of tons)	634	89	1 655	100	161	193
Staple agricultural products (millions of dollars)	6 137	95	13 500	98	120	128

SOURCE: same as for table 9.

efforts toward free trade. Domestic markets alone cannot promote economic development to the same extent. There is already an evident trend to integrate markets. The following chapters will discuss some of the preliminary measures taken toward integration and their scope.

PART TWO

APPROACHES TO

LATIN AMERICAN

ECONOMIC INTEGRATION

CHAPTER 4

GENERAL OUTLINE OF A

LATIN AMERICAN COMMON MARKET

FIRST ATTEMPTS AND DEFINITIONS

Until 1956 a "Latin American common market" had not been specifically mentioned. Although during its first session ECLA adopted a resolution (on June 24, 1948) which spoke of a "Latin American customs union" as a possible subject for discussion, this was not referred to again. From then on, more cautiously, only the possibility of "intensifying" or "increasing intra-Latin American trade" was considered, together with the necessary modifications in trade and payments policies. In 1951, again in ECLA, a Central American proposal was put forth to study measures and programs which would facilitate the intention of that group of countries of integrating their economies and forming "broader markets." No reference was made to a common market or a special customs zone as an aid toward integration. The ECLA resolutions on Central America have always been adopted under the heading of "economic development"—in any event, more logical—and not as a mere aspect of foreign trade.

In November, 1954, at the Extraordinary Meeting of Ministers of Finance or Economy called by the Organization of American States as a result of Resolution LXVI of the Tenth Inter-American Conference, the Secretariat of ECLA and a "preparatory group" of experts presented a report on the problems of development and trade in Latin America.[1] This report used the term "liberalization of inter-Latin American trade" in its analysis of the problem, and it mentioned the need for a "special system" which would not have "the characteristics or the scope of a customs union." It recommended arrangements that, with due regard for existing situations, would seek to stimulate "reciprocal trade in goods which are not at present being produced, which are being manufactured in small quantities or which are only produced on a large scale in some countries and not in others." For such a policy to yield all the anticipated results, "it would have to be of a multilateral character and include the largest possible number of countries." The Preparatory Group, echoing these ideas, also pointed out that direct barter agreements "do not offer the same advantages as the total or partial abolition of customs duties between different countries of the region," and it recommended to the Inter-American Economic and Social Council Conference of Ministers of Finance or Economy a policy of liberalizing "trade between the Latin American countries, reducing or eliminating tariffs and other commercial barriers between them" and of extending "measures initially applied by two or more

---

[1] United Nations, *International Co-operation in a Latin American Development Policy*, Publ. No. 1954, II. 2.

countries to other Latin American nations, including the granting of adequate compensation." [2]

Nevertheless, the 1954 Conference of Ministers of Finance or Economy showed little interest in these proposals, making no mention of them or of the work of ECLA. With only a general reference in the preamble to the importance of intra-Latin American trade—"that it is advisable to take measures to promote regional trade"—a resolution was adopted which recommended to the Inter-American ECOSOC "a study of the possibilities for intensification of regional trade by means of special customs and commercial arrangements between the countries of Latin America." [3]

In 1955, at the opening of the sixth session of ECLA, the latter's Executive Secretary made only this brief statement in reference to a report on intra-Latin American trade: ". . . in addition to making a more detailed analysis of intra-regional trade and its possibilities, [the report] includes a preliminary but very significant analysis of the serious obstacles caused by maritime transport to the development of inter-Latin American trade. All this seems to me to bring us nearer to concrete action, and I cherish the hope that our report will provide a solid basis for the discussion on international trade. . . . Emphasis has been laid on the fact that a policy of import [replacement] must be combined with measures aimed at facilitating intra-Latin American trade. The agreements concluded in this respect in recent years hold out promising prospects, and it is hoped that advantage will be taken of this initial experience to widen the sphere of trade, while simultaneously constructing a progres-

---

[2] *Ibid.*, pp. 72–73, 122, and 142.

[3] Resolution 25 of December 2, 1954. The delegations of Argentina, Mexico, and Uruguay formally expressed their gratitude to ECLA for the studies which had been carried out on this subject (see the Rapporteur's Report of Committee I).

sively multilateral system." [4] Despite this cautious tone, the
delegates to the conference were interested in having the
problem attacked at an intergovernmental level; in their discussions they gave first importance to the necessity of establishing a permanent advisory body and agreed to create the
ECLA Trade Committee[5] "for the purpose of intensifying
inter-Latin American trade . . . through a solution of the
practical problems which hamper or delay such trade and
the preparation of bases to facilitate trade negotiations." [6]
To this end, the Committee, formed by member countries
of ECLA, would concern itself with "the preparation of
specific proposals, in harmony with the present and future
bilateral and multilateral commitments of member governments, and the modifications they may make to them and
taking into consideration national or regional economic conditions," and they would bear in mind "topics . . . such as
the problem of inter-Latin American payments; trade policy;
specific questions of maritime transport and the trade in
given products."

The Trade Committee was set up more than a year
later, in November, 1956, primarily to deal with payments
problems and, only in a relatively secondary way, with the
industrial aspects of expanding intra-Latin American
trade. Two sub-committees were set up, one to examine the
question of payments and the other to study trade in commodities and the possibilities of a "regional market." This
term appeared for the first time in the documents prepared
by the ECLA Secretariat as background information for the

---

[4] Statement of Dr. Raúl Prebisch, executive secretary, at the
plenary session on August 30, 1955. United Nations, ECLA, *Report of the Sixth Session.* New York, October, 1955, Doc.
E/2796/Rev. 1, p. 44.
[5] The idea had been previously taken under consideration, in
1954, during the fifth session of ECLA; but no resolution was
adopted.
[6] Resolution 101 (VI), September 15, 1955.

Committee, and especially in a study presented to that agency by two of its *ad hoc* consultants.[7]

This study, the result of a survey of opinion in seven South American countries, contains a chapter, "The Regional Market," in which the authors present the basic arguments to justify a regional market as a means of accelerating industrialization.[8] Here is today's concept of a common market, to which reference was made in the final section of the preceding chapter. They stated that "the problem of the reform of industrialization within this region —beginning, perhaps, with the group of countries in which industrial progress is most intensive—must be envisaged in terms of wider or more complementary markets, and in a spirit of co-operation reflected in the endeavor to co-ordinate national policies, along the lines exemplified in Europe." And they added, perhaps with too much optimism: "This idea is already very widely accepted." Their conclusion was that "the progressive creation of a large Latin American market would be the only way of solving—by means of complementarity, the improvement of productivity and the consequent increase in consumption—the existing binomial of parallel industries and idle installed capacity." [9]

The consultants' report defined the term "regional market" as "the common trade zone which might be opened up by agreements between more than two countries for specific goods produced by the contracting parties. The

[7] ECLA, *Payments and the Regional Market in Inter-Latin American Trade*, report drafted by José Garrido Torres and Eusebio Campos. (See *Inter-Latin American Trade: Current Problems*, Part II, pp. 93–105.)

[8] A fuller explanation of the ideas of one of the authors, José Garrido Torres, will be found in "Por qué um mercado regional latino-americano?" *Revista Brasileira de Política Internacional*, Año I, No. 2, June, 1959, pp. 74–121.

[9] *Payments and the Regional Market in Inter-Latin American Trade*, p. 98.

agreements would be so drafted as to leave room for the possibility that sooner or later other countries in this region might accede to them." [10] Nevertheless, despite some reference to matters of hemispheric scope the authors were thinking specifically of South America and suggested that it would be wise to evolve gradually toward the wider goal by "beginning in practice with those countries or zones where circumstances are most favourable." They apparently did not consider that intensive industrial progress was taking place, for example, in Mexico. They recommended a "South American economic co-operation programme" which would include: the examination of the possibility of creating industries which require a large amount of capital and broad markets; the conclusion of agreements to implement this program; and the establishment of general principles and specific procedures of trade policy in order to develop gradually a regional, multilateral, and competitive market. The European experiences in the freeing of intraregional trade; the creation of the Coal and Steel Community; and the already imminent Rome Treaty, which in March, 1957, resulted in the establishment of the European Economic Community, were to exert considerable influence on Latin America at this time. The expression "common market" came into use in connection with the prospect of economic integration in Latin America.

Nonetheless, the ECLA Secretariat again showed itself to be extremely cautious, above all about the possibility of achieving a European-type "common market." Its Executive Secretary, in his opening address to the session of the Trade Committee in November, 1956, warned the delegates of the danger of adopting "broad formulae for economic integration," which have failed because they have attempted to "regulate all trade relations between two countries or groups of countries"; and he inquired "if it is

[10] *Ibid.,* p. 100, footnote 14.

not possible to work out more limited arrangements" such as "selecting a number of commodities from industries about to be established or at an early stage, which require expanded markets, and trying to establish systems of industrial reciprocity on the basis of limited schedules." [11] As a personal opinion, he stated that it was necessary to avoid the more general solutions and to consider "a common market for specific commodities." [12] But at the same time he agreed that it was necessary to eliminate payments restrictions that were adversely affecting trade in traditional commodities and to increase trade in raw materials. He recognized that above all Latin American economic integration required a search for "new formulae."

In fact, the Trade Committee considered that the problem was a general Latin American one, not limited just to South America or to specific products. Its Resolution 3 (I), taking into account the need for a more broadly based industrialization, set up a group of experts to complete the studies already carried out, and to project "the possible structure of a regional market designed to contribute to the sound development of Latin American countries, especially those of a basic character, through reduction of costs and the broadening of markets." The group of experts was required: "(a) to define the characteristics of the regional market, bearing in mind the different degrees to which the countries of the region are industri-

---

[11] Statement by Dr. Raúl Prebisch, executive secretary, at the inaugural session held on November 19, 1956. (From mimeographed version of Doc. E/CN.12/C.1/7 Rev. 1, Report of the Trade Committee, First Session. The full report, without the statement, may be found in ECLA, *Inter-Latin American Trade: Current Problems, op. cit.,* Part I).

[12] Note the similarity of the ideas quoted above with those contained in the agreement negotiated between Argentina and Brazil in 1939 (see above, chapter I, p. 21) and with those expressed by ECLA in the document presented to the IA-ECOSOC conference in November, 1954.

alized; (b) to study its possibilities and projections; and (c) to submit recommendations on basic principles and procedures for its establishment."

The discussions and resolutions of the Trade Committee had immediate consequences. First, its recommendation that the central banks form a group of experts to consider the question of multilateral compensation resulted in a meeting of such a working group in May, 1957.[18] Second, in the same month, during its seventh session in La Paz, ECLA took note of the resolutions and held full discussions on the regional market and the payments problem. Third, in August of that year, the OAS Economic Conference in Buenos Aires gave considerable attention to those topics.

At the ECLA meeting, on examination of the report of the Trade Committee, the delegates not only fully supported the work program for the Latin American regional market, but even asked that it be accelerated. Attention was called to the industrial aspects of the market; and the working group set up by the Committee was urged to bear in mind, when drafting its proposals, "the development of a regional market in which consideration would be given to each and every Latin American country." [14] Emphasis was placed on transport problems, payments problems, and restrictions which limit trade in specific commodities. In order to facilitate the task of the governments and to coördinate efforts of ECLA and the Inter-American ECOSOC, the former was requested to transmit to the secretariat of the latter for the Economic Conference of the Organization of American States a complete report on the studies carried out, under way, or scheduled in relation to the creation of a regional market.

A few months later, the views of government representatives attending the Buenos Aires Conference were not

---

[18] See chapter 6.

[14] Resolution 116 (VII), May 27, 1957.

so well defined. At this meeting, consideration was given to documents presented both by ECLA and by the Organization of American States.[15] Some delegations had rather different ideas in mind. For instance, Peru submitted a draft resolution, rather expansive in scope, proposing the establishment of "a permanent inter-American commission for the Western Hemisphere common market." Uruguay suggested that "regional" commissions should be set up "to stimulate trade in each of the economic regions of the Hemisphere," apparently in order to prepare the way for a common market in southern Latin America. Chile recommended "the progressive establishment of a regional market or a free trade area." Argentina, along lines generally similar to those of the two ECLA consultants quoted earlier, supported the continuation of studies on the regional market, but made clear that the latter should be "selective and progressive." Mexico proposed the acceleration of studies to establish "possible bases of agreement for the selective and gradual reduction of tariffs and other restrictions on all inter-Latin American trade," and the subsequent carrying out of "regional conferences" of adjacent countries grouped into "sufficiently large regional zones," in order to determine specific procedures to be followed from then on.

Except for Peru's suggestion, an exclusively Latin American market was envisaged, with simultaneous proposals for "regional markets" [16]—in 1959 being renamed "sub-regional"—and for a single Latin American market or "free trade area." The latter term appeared for the first time and reflected previous thoughts regarding the need to reconcile any future scheme with the GATT provisions.

[15] Among the latter, *Liberalization of Inter-Latin American Trade*, by Raymond F. Mikesell (Pan American Union, Department of Economic and Social Affairs, Washington, D.C., 1957).

[16] This was also the central idea of the OAS Secretariat. See the document cited in footnote 15, especially chapters iv and ix.

The resolution finally adopted set forth in its preamble the considerations that justified a regional market and re-affirmed the idea expressed in La Paz that "all countries of Latin America" be taken into account and that "a broad Latin American market" should be the goal. It also referred to the progress made by the Economic Commission for Latin America in studies on subjects connected with the creation of the Latin American regional market and it recommended that the Inter-American Economic and Social Council take part in such studies after consultation with the ECLA Secretariat.

It is important to stress the expressions "gradually and progressively" and "multilaterally and competitively" in the OAS declaration, because these were to be the basic points of agreement which made it possible to proceed to more specific schemes open to the participation of any interested Latin American country and at the same time in harmony with the GATT policy of multilateralism. By "competitively" it was understood that the creation of monopolies within the regional market would not be favored and that external tariffs would not be imposed at a level which would exclude the commodities of countries outside the area. In later resolutions of the Economic and Social Council and of the General Assembly of the United Nations, these principles were underlined.

GENERAL BASES, STRUCTURE AND FORM

WITHIN THIS FRAMEWORK, at the beginning of 1958 and again in 1959 a group of ECLA experts met to consider and suggest the outlines of a possible common market. This working group divided its study into two parts: first, to propose general bases; and after sufficient time had elapsed for these to be examined and discussed by the governments and public opinion, to make recommendations for the structure and form of the common market. In the second stage, it would appear that the term "common market" had completely replaced "regional market."

The formulation of the general bases[17] was guided by ideas that had been set forth by the Trade Committee and by discussions at previous ECLA and OAS meetings as to the over-all Latin American character that should be given a common market. The working group also recognized that the creation of a European common market was important to Latin America, both as an example and because of its possible adverse effects on Latin American exports of raw materials.

According to this group of experts, membership in the regional market should be open to all Latin American countries, even though countries closely linked by geographical proximity or common economic interests would not be prevented from entering into negotiations among themselves, within the over-all market. The market should also include all goods produced in Latin America, although they might be added progressively and gradually. The less advanced countries should enjoy special advantages in customs tariffs, financing, and other measures, so that they might continue to industrialize and eventually share fully in the regional market. There should be competition within the regional market, and steps were to be taken to prevent unfair practices and monopolistic situations, except where agriculture and certain industries were to be safeguarded.

---

[17] See Report of the First Session of the Working Group, Santiago, Chile, February 3–11, 1958, in ECLA, *The Latin American Common Market,* pp. 28–38.

The participation of private enterprise was felt to be indispensable to the attainment of the aims of the common market.

These were the basic principles. It should be noted that from the beginning it was decided to reject the idea, which had had important support, of limiting the regional market to a few countries or commodities.

As for the form of the regional market, the group of experts clearly advised eventually "adopting a single customs tariff *vis-à-vis* the rest of the world," considering this to be an essential characteristic of a common market. But the group also pointed out that other, often more important, restrictions would have to be eliminated meanwhile, and that, therefore, it envisaged, as an intermediate stage, the possible adoption of a "free trade area," in accordance with the provisions of GATT. Import duties and restrictions within the area would be reduced gradually. Monetary measures would have to include "a special multilateral payments system" in order to realize "the full potential of the market" and to utilize credit balances arising from intra-Latin American trade.[18] A credit system would also be necessary to encourage reciprocal trade and, especially, to promote the export of capital goods. The regional market would also need foreign capital for long-term financing of its new industries and the experts recommended "establishing a special development agency" supplemented by technical assistance. At the same time it urged a study of the different kinds of treatment accorded to private foreign capital.

In its initial proposals, the group of experts made general provisions for such exceptions or safeguards as the right reserved by each country to impose temporary import restrictions for balance of payments reasons or for the purpose of facilitating the readjustment of a national ac-

---

[18] See chapter 6.

tivity which might be adversely affected by the regional market.

The working group, finally, considered that the common market was not yet ready for an "executive authority" as in Europe and that, once in operation, it would need only an advisory body.

A year later, in February, 1959, an enlarged working party with access to more numerous and complete documentation made more detailed recommendations to the governments on the system that should be adopted for the creation of a Latin American common market and on policies necessary to put it into effect. It was expected that these recommendations would be approved at the eighth session of ECLA, soon to be held in Panama City, and that the Secretariat could then prepare "an initial common market draft agreement."

The working group then made clear[19] that the common market would be, strictly speaking, an ultimate objective. It would have to go through a preliminary stage of ten years. During this period a free-trade zone would be established in which duties and other restrictions affecting the greater part of intra-Latin American trade would be gradually reduced. That is, there would be no question of equalizing external customs duties during the ten year period, but only of progressively reducing those in force between the parties to the agreement.

Within the first year, a uniform percentage reduction would be applied to each of the customs and similar taxes on imports; within five years, quantitative restrictions would be eliminated or converted into import taxes; and over the ten-year period, the average levels of import taxes would be systematically reduced. Nevertheless, the experts pro-

---

[19] *Report of the Second Session of the Working Group (Mexico City, 16 to 27 February 1959).* See ECLA, *The Latin American Common Market,* pp. 38–50.

posed that the reductions be differentiated among three categories of products: (*i*) on primary goods, import taxes and restrictions would be entirely abolished, with certain exceptions; (*ii*) on capital goods, motor vehicles, other durable goods, intermediate products, and others for which demand tends to grow intensively or for which a large import replacement margin exists, import taxes would be reduced to "the lowest possible average"; and (*iii*) on manufactured goods for which demand tends to grow slowly or which are already being produced in almost all the countries, a "more moderate" reduction of taxes would be applied. In the last two categories, the adoption of *averages* as targets for reduction of import taxes would make the system sufficiently flexible to allow for more or less progress according to the type of product.

In order to facilitate, through special concessions, and encourage the industrialization of the less developed countries, there would be three groups of members: (a) countries of more advanced development in the products of categories (*ii*) and (*iii*); (b) countries of advanced development in the products of category (*ii*); and (c) countries of incipient development in the products of category (*iii*) and still undeveloped in the other categories.

In order to promote industrial complementarity or specialization, it was provided that countries linked by geographical proximity or common economic interests could agree upon reductions or abolitions of import taxes which would not have to be automatically extended to the other members of the region. It was also recognized that existing preferential concessions could only be eliminated gradually and that the Central American common market might be considered an economic unit within the region.

The original recommendation that the regional market include all interested Latin American countries was maintained, but it was recognized that a smaller group of countries might launch the market, provided that all countries of Latin America would be invited to the initial negotiations and that the others could sign the agreement at a later date. Finally, the working group agreed that for the administration of the agreement, it would be necessary to set up a central body to be called the Committee on Trade Policy and Payments, composed of representatives of all member countries.

The experts also recommended some basic principles to ensure the successful development of the free-trade region. The first of these was the principle of reciprocity conceived of as equivalent *increases* in trade, which would compel countries to take additional action in order to increase their imports from the region to the same extent that they increased their exports to it. This principle is implicitly related to multilateral payments compensations, so far as the latter may be necessary, since with general currency convertibility it would not be indispensable to balance trade within the region.

Other important principles contained in the proposals referred to the coördination of trade policy toward the rest of the world and the equalizing of external tariffs when differences in tariff levels might prevent establishment of an adequate margin of preference within the region. As in the previous year, the experts included recommendations on credit and financing, rules of competition, safeguards, participation of private enterprise, and made new suggestions on determination of the origin of goods, standard customs nomenclature, statistics, and the like. One member of the working group pointed out that the recommendations should stipulate specific dates or periods for the complete liberalization of trade within the common market, so as not to give the impression that a mere preferential trading area was being proposed; and he objected to the provisions for special agreements to reduce tariffs on particular commodities which would not be extended to all member countries.

Although the working-group session was to be shortly followed in May by the Trade Committee session, experts from the four southern countries—Argentina, Brazil, Chile, and Uruguay—met together meanwhile for consultations on trade policy and drafted a proposal similar in some respects to that of the working group. These consultants had previously, in August, 1958, considered means of liberalizing trade between their countries, but they did not take under discussion tariff barriers. On the later occasion, they included this topic and drafted a proposal for a free-trade area which would be acceptable under the terms of GATT and that, at least nominally, might constitute the initial group of countries mentioned by the working group (although no other country was invited to send experts to participate in those negotiations). On the other hand, this proposal differed from the recommendations of the working group by stipulating stages for progressively reducing the averages of duties; it did not classify products in different categories; and it did not provide clearly and fully for the possible situation of member countries whose level of industrial development might entitle them to special treatment. Moreover, the proposal was only thought of as a provisional instrument to solve urgent problems arising from the approaching termination of bilateral agreements between the four countries.[20]

This was the background of the ECLA meeting held in Panama City in May, 1959. The Trade Committee agreed to use the documents of the working group as the basis for discussions and only to take note of information provided by the report of the four southern-zone countries. Nonetheless, both proposals were present in all discussions and although the resolution that was adopted incorporated

---

[20] The draft free-trade area is examined in chapter 5.

mainly the ideas of the working group, actually the prevailing unofficial opinion was that the southern-zone proposal was more feasible so long as other countries were invited to join and certain important points were incorporated, such as the special situation of the less developed countries. In the conference, emphasis was laid on the need to avoid the formation of exclusive "sub-regional" groups —except for the Central American—and to try to make the Latin American common market as broad in scope as possible.[21] On the other hand, several specific recommendations of the working group were rejected by some important delegations and by representatives of GATT and the International Monetary Fund; and some countries stated that they would only be in a position to consider entering the common market after a long and thorough study.

The most significant decision of the Trade Committee, supported by the plenary ECLA Commission, was to invite the governments to set up a group of high-ranking experts which would hold its first session within a few months and would prepare a preliminary draft agreement on the Latin American common market; the preliminary draft would be transmitted to the governments for study and then to the ECLA Trade Committee for preparation of the final draft agreement.[22] At the same time, the Committee recommended the following general principles for the setting up of the common market:

a) To include all the Latin American countries which decide to participate in its formation;
b) To remain open to the accession of other Latin American countries;

---

[21] The report of the proceedings of the second session of the Trade Committee is found in ECLA, *The Latin American Common Market*, pp. 111–135.

[22] Resolution 6 (II), May 19, 1959.

c) To operate on competitive bases and comprise the largest
possible number of products;

d) To take into consideration the inequalities that exist
among the Latin American countries in so far as their economic development is concerned;

e) To be characterized by the progressive standardization of
the customs tariffs and other instruments of trade policy
of the Latin American countries, in their relations with
other areas, due allowance being made for international
commitments;

f) To depend, for its realization, on the widest possible collaboration on the part of private enterprise;

g) To promote increasing specialization in economic activities, in order to improve utilization of factors of production available in the region; and

h) To contribute to the expansion and diversification of
trade among the Latin American countries, and between
them and the rest of the world.

From that moment, events moved swiftly. The draft
of the southern-zone countries was broadened, under the
influence of the general principles recently laid down by
the Trade Committee. This made it possible for Bolivia,
Paraguay, and Peru to participate in the new negotiations
with Argentina, Brazil, Chile, and Uruguay. As a result of
these negotiations, in September, 1959, the proposal for a
free-trade area was drawn up by the group of seven countries, and in February, 1960, with the incorporation of
Mexico, the Latin American Free Trade Association was
created by the Montevideo Treaty. This agreement was
open to the accession of other countries. The work program
adopted by the Trade Committee at its Panama meeting
was thus greatly modified and abbreviated by far-reaching
decisions taken by the governments. A discussion of the
background of the Montevideo Treaty and the characteristics of the free-trade area which it establishes follows
in the next chapter.

CHAPTER 5

CREATION OF A FREE-TRADE AREA

THE PROPOSALS

It has been mentioned that the studies and general recommendations related to a possible Latin American common market always admitted the idea that such a market might be initiated by a group of countries linked by geographical proximity or common economic interests. Since eight Latin American countries, including those most interested in forming the common market, belonged to GATT, it was thought that, under one of the exceptions permitted by the general agreement as in the case of the European Coal and Steel Community, a formula might be found whereby the most-favored-nation clause would not apply in the free-trade area for countries outside the area.

It was proposed not to create a series of "sub-regional" agreements which would later merge into a single "Latin American regional" agreement, but to take advantage of the initiative of a few important countries in order to incorporate others later and so create the nucleus of the future common market. Four countries, Argentina, Brazil, Chile and Uruguay, led the way. Because of bilateral-payments problems and a 25 per cent reduction in trade carried out through compensation accounts between 1955 and 1957, these countries were anxious to reach a multilateral arrangement which would liberalize their reciprocal trade and facilitate the settlement of balances resulting from monetary agreements.

In August, 1958, experts from the four governments met at ECLA headquarters for consultation on a program of liberalization of trade barriers other than customs tariffs; but they agreed that "rapid and resolute steps must be taken to establish an intraregional preferential customs tariff," which would impart substance and stability to the liberalization measures.[1] Such a preferential tariff would constitute "a decisive step towards economic integration arrangements of wider scope, such as a free trade zone or customs union." The group concluded that it would be necessary to invoke the provisions of the GATT Charter, under Article XXV, in order to institute a "Latin American exception" to the most-favored-nation clause. In order not to limit the proposal to the interests of the four countries represented, the experts requested the ECLA Secretariat to prepare as soon as possible a memorandum summing up the principles and objectives of a Latin American preferential tariff system which might later lead to the institution

---

[1] Summary record of the meetings held at the headquarters of ECLA, Santiago, Chile, 26 August to 1 September 1958. See ECLA, *Consultations on Trade Policy*, Doc. E/CN.12/C.1/11, March 28, 1959.

of one of the systems envisaged in GATT.[2] Finally, it was recommended that the experts on their own account should ask their governments—of the four, only Argentina was not a member of GATT—to present to the contracting parties of the agreement a communication requesting approval of the establishment of an intra-Latin American preferential tariff in accordance with the terms of the General Agreement, Article XXV, paragraph (5)*a*,[3] under which the obligations imposed on a group of countries by the most-favored-nation clause may be waived by a two-thirds majority.

In November, 1959, the Brazilian and Chilean representatives to the thirteenth session of GATT informed the other parties of their intention to submit for consideration at a later date a specific proposal to set up a preferential trade zone in Latin America. It was arranged, in consultation with the Executive Secretariat of GATT, to postpone deciding under which exception of the agreement the proposal would be presented; but Article XXIV began to be regarded as the most appropriate for the creation of a free-trade area.

Therefore, when the experts of Argentina, Brazil, Chile, and Uruguay met again for consultations with the Secretariat at ECLA headquarters in April 1959, it was decided to choose the formula of a "free trade area." [4] Article XXIV of GATT[5] provides that, between two or more customs territories, duties and other restrictive regulations of commerce may be eliminated on "substantially all" the trade in products originating in such territories,

---

[2] *Ibid.*, paragraphs 15 and 16.
[3] *Ibid.*, paragraph 18.
[4] See the *Summary Record* of the meeting, Santiago, April 6 to 16, 1959, in ECLA, *The Latin American Common Market*, pp. 93–108.
[5] *General Agreement on Tariffs and Trade*, Geneva, 1958.

and that the constituent territories shall not be required to maintain uniform duties with the rest of the world, so long as the corresponding duties imposed on the trade of countries outside the area shall not be higher than those existing before the formation of the free-trade area. Moreover, any interim agreement between the contracting parties leading to the formation of a free-trade area shall include a plan and a schedule for the formation of such a free-trade area within a reasonable length of time. Any member of GATT deciding to enter in a free-trade area shall promptly notify the other parties so that the latter may make such reports and recommendations as they may deem appropriate. Of the four countries which proposed the Latin American free-trade area, only Argentina, as already stated, was not a member of GATT.

This draft agreement on a free-trade area began with a declaration of principles in which it was stated that a solution was sought to the urgent problems affecting reciprocal trade between the parties. In addition, it was considered that the free-trade area would be a good starting point for those efforts aimed at the formation of the Latin American common market. The contracting parties, therefore, declared their readiness to renegotiate this agreement with the participation of as many Latin American countries as possible, as soon as there was a concurrence of views on the specific solutions. Meanwhile the agreement would remain open for accession by any other Latin American country; and "provision" was made for the adoption of special measures favoring the less developed countries. It was stated that the agreement should be applied not only to existing trade but to future industrial activities and that it would be an instrument directed toward economic integration. At the same time, it would conform to "the fundamental principles of existing instruments which govern international trade"—that is, GATT—and it would in no way follow a policy of isolation which would only be detrimental to the foreign trade of member countries.

The objective of the agreement was to establish a free trade area within ten years, during which the parties would gradually eliminate the duties and other restrictions imposed on the reciprocal trade in products originating in their territories. Such measures of elimination would be applied to "substantially all" the trade between the parties. The liberalization would be achieved by annual negotiations—based on reciprocity of concessions—which would result in lowering each year by 8 per cent cumulatively the weighted average of the duties applying to countries outside the zone at the time the agreement entered into force. This system would be sufficiently flexible to permit each country to make initial concessions that would be greater for some products than for others, always provided that the 8 per cent average reduction was arrived at. Nevertheless, the agreement also provided that by the end of the third year the member countries should have completely eliminated charges and other restrictions on products whose value would amount to 25 per cent of their intraregional trade; by the end of the sixth year it would amount to 50 per cent; by the ninth year to 75 per cent; and a year later to 80 per cent. In this way it would be possible to achieve gradually the required goal of substantially all trade, and the program would not stop half-way. Although the parties were not required to maintain uniform customs duties with the rest of the world, it was realized that a disparity of such duties for some products or their raw materials might give rise to difficulties. Therefore, it was provided that the parties should endeavor to conciliate their export and import regimes, as well as the fiscal and exchange procedures applied to the rest of the world. The most-favored-nation treatment would be granted as between all contracting parties, without discrimination.

There was no classification of products either for purposes of customs negotiations or of indicating the extent to which they should be liberalized. However, safeguard clauses were provided that would permit quantitative restrictions on imports of items intended "to complement basic domestic products which are important for the national economy or which are included in special programs promoted by the Government, always provided that such restrictions do not signify a reduction in the effective consumption capacity of the importing country." Exports might also be restricted in order to ensure the domestic supply of specific products. The programs for producing, importing, and exporting the restricted items would be coördinated so as to maintain traditional trade levels. In addition, special protective temporary measures might be adopted because of the balance-of-payments situation or because of unforeseen factors or serious maladjustments.

The position of the relatively less developed countries which might accede to the agreement was only considered by empowering the parties "to grant exclusive concessions to other contracting parties in order to expedite the development of specific lines of production." On the other hand, it was considered that there might be exceptions which would not be extended to all the products or to all the member countries, "by virtue of specific agreements negotiated . . . for the purposes of industrial complementarity."

The free-trade area would be administered by a Trade and Payments Committee composed of representatives of the member governments and having its own secretariat. The Committee would make use of the technical advice of ECLA and would arrange for the collaboration of any other national or international organizations. It would be at the same time the vehicle for negotiations of multilateral payments agreements and the sole administrator of such agreements or arrangements. The payments system regarded as suitable was that based on the multilateral compensation of bilateral balances recommended by the Meeting of Central Banks and contained in the so-called Rio de Janeiro Protocol, which will be discussed later.[6]

The proposal of a free-trade area by the four southern-zone countries was noted during the second session of the Trade Committee held in Panama in May, 1959. At the same time, consideration was given to the recommendations of the working group, which had done a parallel study of the bases and structure of a Latin American common market.[7] The advanced stage reached by the four southern-zone countries in their negotiations gave rise to concern in other countries, including Cuba, Mexico, and Peru, that a sub-regional market might be created in the South which would prove an impediment to the later establishment of a broader market. Nevertheless, the Trade Committee was not empowered to object to any special arrangement concluded by a number of countries in the exercise of their sovereignty. As pointed out in chapter 4, the Committee limited itself to setting forth what it believed should be the general bases for a common market and it decided to recommend that member governments set up a group of high-ranking experts which would meet not later than February, 1960.

There is no doubt that these considerations influenced the final drafting of the proposal of the southern-zone countries, and the timing of the later steps taken toward a common market. In June, 1959, with Bolivia, Paraguay, and Peru also invited, a consultative meeting of experts from Argentina, Brazil, Chile, and Uruguay was held in Lima.

---

[6] See chapter 6, which also reviews steps taken earlier with respect to the payments problem.

[7] In September, 1958, an unofficial meeting of the foreign ministers of the American republics was held in Washington. One of the statements made was that practical measures should be adopted to intensify efforts toward the establishment of "regional markets" in Latin America.

Uruguay then convened a diplomatic conference for the purpose of concluding a treaty to establish a free-trade zone between the seven countries. These negotiations, which were carried out at Montevideo in September, 1959, and to which Mexico and Venezuela were invited to send observers, resulted in a proposal of a free-trade-zone treaty to be ratified in February, 1960. In December, 1959, the representatives of the central banks were to meet again to consider the payments problem which had been left pending, and amendments to the free-trade-zone proposal were to be accepted until January 15. The meeting on payments was actually held in January, 1960, but no conclusion was reached. However, the treaty proposal was again examined in February; this time Mexico, which had been invited to accede a month before, also took part. The treaty was signed on February 18, 1960, by the foreign ministers of the participating countries, except Bolivia.

Meanwhile, in October, 1959, six Latin American countries—Argentina, Bolivia, Brazil, Chile, Peru, and Uruguay (the last four as members of GATT)—had notified the fifteenth session of GATT, for purposes of information, that they intended to set up a Latin American free-trade area in accordance with the proposal drawn up in September and which they considered to be consistent with the provisions of Article XXIV of the General Agreement.[8] It was also stated that the final text would be presented to the parties of GATT at a later date. In December, 1959, moreover, during its fourteenth session, the United Nations General Assembly unanimously adopted a resolution on the Latin American common market in which it expressed the hope that this market would "help to expand and diversify trade among the Latin American countries

---

[8] The six-country declaration may be found in *Suplemento al Boletín Quincenal*, Centro de Estudios Monetarios Latinoamericanos, Mexico, November, 1959, p. 330.

and between them and other regions of the world, and to accelerate their national and regional economic development.[9]

THE MONTEVIDEO TREATY[10]

UNDER THIS TREATY, signed in February, 1960, by the governments of Argentina, Bolivia,[11] Brazil, Chile, Mexico, Peru, and Uruguay, a free-trade area was established and a Latin American Free-Trade Association was organized, with headquarters in Montevideo.[12] The treaty makes no mention of the circumstantial reasons for the original proposal of the four southern-zone countries; however it clearly establishes that the objective is to achieve gradually and progressively a Latin American common market and to favor the complementation and integration of the economies of the member countries. In addition, special attention is given to the situation of the relatively less developed countries. In its other aspects, the treaty follows the lines of the proposal

---

[9] General Assembly of the United Nations, Fourteenth Session, Resolution 1430 (XIV), December 5, 1959.

[10] See its text in Appendix B.

[11] Bolivia, which did not sign in Montevideo, was granted a moratorium until June 18, 1960 to accede to the treaty as a signatory state. This time limit was subsequently extended, but by the time the treaty went into force on June 1, 1961, Bolivia had not yet decided to form part of the Latin American Free-Trade Association. On the other hand, Colombia and Ecuador announced in May, 1961, their decision to subscribe to the treaty.

[12] The term "association" corresponds to that used by seven European countries—Austria, Denmark, Norway, Portugal, the United Kingdom, Sweden, and Switzerland——for the free-trade area which they set up among themselves. The common market of the other six—Germany, Belgium, France, Italy, Luxemburg, and the Netherlands—is officially known as the European Economic Community.

for a free-trade area suggested in April, 1959, by experts of four of the mentioned countries.

The treaty stipulates a period of twelve years, instead of the ten years provided for in the original proposal, from the date of the treaty's entry into force, during which the parties shall gradually eliminate from substantially all their reciprocal trade the duties, charges, and other such restrictions on the imports of goods originating in the territory of any contracting party. By duties and charges is meant "customs duties and any other charges of equivalent effect— whether fiscal, monetary or exchange—that are levied on imports." Annual negotiations shall be conducted in order to reduce the duties and charges by 8 per cent of the weighted average applicable to countries outside the area. "National schedules" will be drawn up of the negotiated products; these concessions may be withdrawn by negotiation and on the basis of adequate compensation. A "common schedule" will also be prepared and will consist of products on which duties, charges, and restrictions will be completely eliminated; this schedule should represent 25 per cent of the value of the trade between the parties by the end of three years, 50 per cent by the end of six years, 75 per cent by the end of nine years, and "substantially all of such trade" during the third three-year period. The concessions granted in the Common Schedule will be irrevocable. The treaty provides a method for calculation of the percentages.

The treaty refers to the so-called "principle of reciprocity," which apparently can be interpreted in two ways: on the one hand, as reciprocity of concessions, that is, no unilateral or inequitable concessions shall be granted; on the other hand, as the "expected growth in the flow of trade" between each party and the others as a whole, with respect to the negotiated products. It is not necessary that imports of each country from the rest of the area should be equal to its exports; but if the concessions should result in "significant and persistent" disadvantages for a country, a study will be made of the problem in order to adopt measures designed to promote trade at the highest possible levels. Such measures should not be restrictive. If the disparity of the levels of the duties, charges, and restrictions is very great, negotiations, based on reciprocity of concessions, will be conducted with due consideration for equity. Moreover, an effort will be made to reconcile the import and export systems, as well as the treatments accorded to capital, goods, and services from outside the area. With the exception of border trade, each party shall avoid discrimination in its treatment of the products of the others. In theory and practice, the aim will be to increase trade, not to limit it.

The treaty includes and explicitly justifies the safeguarding clauses which had been presented in previous proposals. Nondiscriminatory restrictions may be imposed when the imports of negotiated products "have or are liable to have serious repercussions" on specific productive activities of vital importance, and when they are designed to correct an unfavorable over-all balance of payments. But all these restrictions should be temporary and, if prolonged for more than one year, should be eliminated through negotiations.

Provisions for the conclusion of special agreements of complementation and integration are set forth more clearly and fully than in any of the preceding proposals. The parties shall endeavor to promote progressively closer coördination of the corresponding industrial policies and may negotiate mutual agreements on complementarity by industrial sectors. These arrangements shall set forth the special "liberalization program" to be applied to commodities of the sector concerned, including clauses intended to harmonize the treatments accorded to raw materials and other components used in the manufacture of these products. No country wishing to participate shall be excluded from these agreements. In agriculture, special arrangements are also permitted. The parties shall seek to coördinate their policies of agricultural development and of trade in agricultural commodities. But they may also limit imports of the latter in order to regulate internal production and supplies, provided that measures are taken to expand intra-area trade in these commodities.

The situation of economically less advanced countries which accede to the treaty is presented in a special chapter. The parties shall endeavor to create conditions conducive to the economic growth of those countries. To this end, the parties may: authorize a country to grant exclusive advantages to another country which is at a relatively less advanced stage of economic development; authorize the latter country to implement the program for the reduction of duties, charges, and other restrictions "under more favorable conditions" (that is, less rapidly or intensively), and permit it to adopt appropriate measures to correct an unfavorable balance of payments or to protect its domestic output. In addition, it will be the collective responsibility of the parties to support, both inside and outside the area, financial and technical measures designed to bring about the expansion of existing productive activities in a country at a less advanced stage of development, and to promote special technical assistance programs intended to raise productivity in specific production sectors of a country in that situation. In a protocol to the treaty, it was stated that Bolivia and Paraguay "are at present in a position to invoke in their favor the provisions in the treaty concerning special treatment for countries at a relatively less advanced stage of economic development." [13]

---

[13] Ecuador has also requested to be permitted to accede to the treaty as a country at a relatively less advanced stage of development.

Unlike the original draft proposal of the four southern-zone countries, the treaty specifies that the Free-Trade Association shall have two organs. The supreme organ will be the Conference composed of duly accredited representatives of the member governments. It shall adopt all decisions of importance and shall meet once a year, or, if necessary, more often. During the first two years its decisions shall be adopted when affirmative votes are cast by at least two-thirds of the parties, and providing that no negative vote is cast. The other organ will be the Standing Executive Committee, consisting of a permanent representative of each government. It will be responsible for supervising the implementation of the provisions of the treaty and for undertaking, with the aid of a technical secretariat, studies of problems which may arise. As in the United Nations agencies, the secretariat will be strictly impartial.

The treaty contains other miscellaneous provisions concerning freedom of transit, subsidies, measures relating to the protection of a nation's cultural heritage, health, and so on, and concerning its entry into force. The treaty is of unlimited duration, but any party wishing to withdraw from it may do so by advising the other parties one year in advance; however, all concessions relating to reductions in duties, charges, and other restrictions received or granted by it under the liberalization program shall remain in force for five years. On the other hand, the treaty will remain open to accession by the other Latin American states, on condition that the acceding state accepts the existing reciprocal concessions in the area and carries out the minimum obligations accumulated during the period since the entry into force of the treaty.

Finally, the treaty shall be considered as an instrument which directs the liberalization of trade between the parties toward the ultimate establishment of a Latin American common market. The parties shall make "every effort to direct

their policies with a view to creating conditions favorable"
to that end. On the expiry of twelve years from the entry
into force of the treaty, the parties shall proceed to study
the results of the treaty's implementation and "shall initiate the necessary collective negotiations with a view to
fulfilling more effectively the purposes of the Treaty and,
if desirable, to adapting it to a new stage of economic integration."

Although the payments questions was not solved before the Montevideo meeting, it was not considered that this
would interfere with the organization of the Free-Trade
Association, and it was decided to convene further meetings
of experts from the central banks of the member countries
in order to continue the studies on payments and credits.
The present situation of this problem, as well as its background, is discussed in the following chapter.

CHAPTER 6

PROPOSALS FOR MULTILATERAL

PAYMENTS COMPENSATION

SINCE THE Montevideo Treaty did not solve the problem of multilateral payments compensation between the Latin American countries, this problem is still open to discussion. It is, therefore, useful to examine the manner in which this aspect of the freeing of intra-Latin American trade has evolved and to evaluate the present situation.

As mentioned, in 1956 the Trade Committee of ECLA undertook to find ways out of the rigid and complex system of bilateral agreements. The discussions at its first meeting gave promise of solving the payments problem even before the common market was worked out. A detailed resolution on payments was adopted by the Committee.[1] On the one hand, it invited the central banks or monetary authorities

[1] Resolution 1 (I), adopted on November 28, 1956.

of the Latin American countries having bilateral agreements
to set up a working group which would study the possibility of "gradually establishing a multilateral payments regime" and would suggest measures calculated to achieve
that end. On the other hand, it took note of the fact that
during the period before such a regime could be achieved
the mentioned countries were interested in giving greater
flexibility to their payments relations and in adopting basic
principles which were specified as follows:

a) Equal quotations for units of account and convertible currencies on the exchange markets concerned, for the same
   operations;
b) Trade at prices not higher than those prevailing on the
   world market. If no bases for comparison are available,
   quotations shall not exceed prices paid by any third country under the same conditions;
c) Payment through the agreement-accounts of the following items, *inter alia:*
   (i) the value of traded commodities;
   (ii) freight charges relating to direct traffic;
   (iii) insurance and re-insurance;
   (iv) other expenditures accessory to trade;
   (v) other items agreed upon by the contracting parties;
d) Reciprocal credits adequate for the satisfactory development of trade, due allowance being made for seasonal
   fluctuations;
e) Automatic transfers to the accounts of other countries
   participating in the system of transfer of balances, through
   communication with the Central Bank of the debtor country, of sums in excess of the stipulated swing credits;
f) Reciprocal transfer of the above-mentioned countries' accounts of favorable balances between the Central Banks
   concerned.

Furthermore, the countries were willing "in order to
facilitate the voluntary reciprocal transfer of the balances in

these accounts . . . to exchange information periodically and opportunely, through the appropriate central banks . . . on the state of the clearing accounts in force between the countries concerned," and, should a special machinery be required to facilitate this task, they would request the coöperation of the secretariats of ECLA and of the International Monetary Fund.

The meeting of the Working Group of Central Banks was held in Montevideo in May, 1957, and was attended by representatives of eight South American countries. The principal result of this meeting was the drafting of a proposal for a standard bilateral agreement as a preliminary to multilateralization, in order to bring into harmony the scope, terminology, and provisions of the different existing bilateral agreements. Among the main points of agreement were, in addition to uniform terminology and content, the adoption of the United States dollar as an accounting unit, the inclusion of freight and insurance in payments to be settled through the bilateral accounts, and the right to demand (with respect to balances in excess of a certain amount), repayment in dollars or in other freely convertible currencies or transfer of these balances to another existing account. It was also decided to submit to the ECLA Secretariat data on bilateral positions which would be transmitted to the other central banks. This was to enable the latter, if they so wished, to carry out triangular or multilateral settlements.

The standard agreement was adopted shortly afterward by Argentina, Bolivia, Chile, and Uruguay and it was instrumental in simplifying and unifying the functioning of payments with regard to a substantial share of intra-Latin American trade. It also made possible a measure of transferability.

At the end of 1958 a second meeting of the Working Group of Central Banks was held in Rio de Janeiro, with sixteen countries represented, in order to enter a new stage and study the possibility of establishing a compensation center which might ultimately become a Latin American Payments Union. The proposal made for multilateral compensation of bilateral balances provided for participation in the system by any Latin American country which held two or more accounts based on the standard agreement. Two types of compensations would be carried out, through the agency of the ECLA Secretariat: "first-category compensations" intended to reduce one or more of the debit balances held by each party, that is, to result in a balancing of the system; and "second-category compensations" intended to transfer balances from one account to another, but within the corresponding bilateral credit margins. First-category compensation would be automatic, but second-category compensations would require the consent of the central banks holding the accounts that would be affected. Provisions were also included to permit omission of some amounts from the balances to be settled in first category, and other elements of flexibility were introduced.

This system, according to the proposal, was to take effect at once but it was also felt necessary to put forth a temporary system so that countries which did not hold bilateral accounts could take part in the multilateralization of settlements. It was emphasized that the adoption of this compensation system would be only another step toward the regional market and increasing intra-Latin American trade. The proposals were set forth in the form of a draft protocol [2] to be signed as part of the more general arrangements, or even before. No specific recommendation was made on a possible payments union except to suggest to governments that they consider the creation of a special international agency.

---

[2] ECLA, *Report of the Second Session of the Central Banks Working Group*, annex to Doc. E/CN.12/C.1/10. The text can also be found in ECLA, *The Latin American Common Market*, pp. 106–107.

The Trade Committee did not discuss the proposal for multilateral compensation until its second session in May, 1959, which took place at the same time as the eighth session of ECLA held in Panama; but in April, 1959, during the consultations held between experts of Argentina, Brazil, Chile, and Uruguay at the ECLA headquarters, it was concluded that, in view of the urgent need to solve difficult bilateral situations and of the termination at an early date of the respective agreements, it was advisable to recommend to those four governments that they sign a treaty to create a free-trade area. This agreement—whose terms were analyzed in the preceding chapter—included provisions on payments. The experts considered that those provisions were fully covered by the Rio de Janeiro Protocol on compensations. They went even further when they stated that "their respective countries had decided to join the system, and the internal requisites for their accession had just been duly complied with" and that, in order to formalize the agreement, all that was necessary—in the absence of an autonomous international instrument—was to address communications to the ECLA Secretariat in which the central banks would state that they agreed "to participate in the operations for the multilateral compensation of bilateral balances provided for in the draft protocol." [3]

However, the draft protocol on multilateral compensation did not go into effect. On the other hand, a related draft proposal, that of the four southern-zone countries for a free-trade area, evolved as has already been seen until in February, 1960, it became the Montevideo Treaty, still without providing any solution to the payments problem.

The difficulties about payments multilateralization have arisen because the initial four countries expanded to

---

[3] Summary Record of the consultations on trade policy held at ECLA Headquarters (6–16 April, 1959). See *The Latin American Common Market*, pp. 99 and 106.

include another four, two of which—Mexico and Peru—have convertible currencies and very little experience with bilateral balances or multilateral arrangements. Another source of difficulties has been the insistent objections of the International Monetary Fund to any Latin American system of regional multilateral compensation which would require or entail forming a payments union. Furthermore, when it was decided to create the free-trade zone under the Montevideo Treaty it was seen more clearly that the problem of payments transferability among members led to the more complex one of the granting of credits to facilitate trade within the zone.

During the second session of ECLA's Trade Committee held in Panama, the doctrinal objections of the International Monetary Fund were publicly stated. Although the proposals of the central bank experts and of the ECLA Secretariat were supported by most Latin American delegates, representatives of the International Monetary Fund and of the United States and the United Kingdom did not think it advisable to try to establish a payments union. The Monetary Fund considered that a payments union was neither a necessary nor a desirable instrument for the formation of the common market; and that it would prolong or perpetuate bilateralism since it would mean that even countries without bilateral accounts would have to adopt and maintain them or establish exchange controls. According to the Fund, the trend toward general convertibility would make a compensations mechanism superfluous. On the other hand, the ECLA Secretariat insisted that the convertibility of several Latin American currencies was more apparent than real, since it was maintained with the help of heavy import restrictions such as prior import deposits and surcharges; therefore, a payments union would make possible real convertibility. Far from requiring bilateral agreements, the compensations system would need only registered ledger accounts. The purpose of the system would be to facilitate and extend regional trade.[4] As may be seen, the Fund disagreed with the supporters of a multilateral compensations system not only as to the possibility of carrying out multilateral settlements or the ability of countries to try to work out among themselves their payments problems, but also as to the advisability of establishing a *permanent system* of compensation and a regional *payments union* as a corresponding instrument which would include credit provisions. In the brief time available to the meeting of the Trade Committee these problems were not finally settled and it was agreed to ask the ECLA Secretariat and the International Monetary Fund to continue studying them.

Shortly thereafter considerable progress was made toward the creation of a Latin American free-trade zone and, as a result of the draft prepared in Montevideo in September, 1959, a meeting of representatives of central banks was convened to consider the payments problem once again before final negotiation and signing of the treaty on free trade. The payments meeting took place in February, 1960, attended by delegates of Argentina, Bolivia, Brazil, Chile, Paraguay, Peru, and Uruguay, as well as by observers from Colombia, Ecuador, Mexico, and Panama and experts from ECLA, the International Monetary Fund, and other organizations. By that time, Peru had entered into the free-trade-area proposals and held the opinion that there should be no limit on free convertibility of intra-Latin American trade balances. Peru's position differed from that of countries like Mexico, which had announced its intention of joining the area and which accepted the idea of establishing a compensations system and of appointing an agency for registration of transactions so long as the general converti-

---

[4] On the above, see *Report of the Second Session of the Trade Committee*, in ECLA, *The Latin American Common Market*, pp. 123–124.

bility of its own currency were not affected; from that of countries like Argentina and Chile, which wished to avoid bilateralism, but maintained currency convertibility by means of drastic import restrictions that could not be lifted with regard to other Latin American countries without a multilateralization of regional payments; and from that of Brazil which, because of its general foreign-exchange situation, could only gradually abandon its bilateral accounts in favor of a system of multilateral compensation.

ECLA presented proposals to introduce the granting of *reciprocal credit facilities* into a system of payments compensation in order to make possible the expansion of Latin American trade and to multilateralize the persistent debtor or creditor positions of single countries toward the other members of the area.[5] One of the proposals was in substance an automatic multilateral compensation system with a central agency. At regular intervals this agency would determine in dollar units of account the balances maintained with it by each of the central banks and would proceed to settle those balances. Certain proportions of the balances under existing bilateral agreements could also be transferred to the multilateral system. The debtor and creditor positions resulting from the consolidation of the balances—and the automatic credit implied by the existence of balances that would not have to be settled immediately—would be an incentive to increased trade between the countries of the zone. At no time would intra-Latin American trade be interrupted on account of exchange shortages. Furthermore, since intraregional trade would not require all payments to be made in dollars, such dollar savings or economies would become available for transactions with the rest of the world.

---

[5] ECLA, *Payments and Credits in the Free-Trade Area Projected by Latin American Countries. Possible Systems.* Working Paper No. 1, October 30, 1959 (recently reproduced in ECLA, *Papers on Financial Problems Prepared . . . for the Latin American Free-Trade Association,* E/CN.12/569, March 1, 1961).

But automatic credit would have to be limited by agreement, and beyond that limit settlements would have to be effected in convertible currency.

ECLA called this payments formula a system of *"a priori* credits." But in case of objections, ECLA offered an alternative system of *"a posteriori* credits" which would permit some transactions to take place in dollars and which would be much less automatic. This alternative would be of greater practical interest to countries which, because of their convertible currencies, would tend to earn balances payable in dollars in their trade with the others. Under this system, each country would grant to the central agency a credit in dollar units of account and would receive one from it in return. Reciprocal transactions currently paid for in dollars would be communicated periodically to the compensations agency by each central bank. The latter would also at regular intervals report to the agency all transactions relating to existing bilateral accounts and would transfer to the agency for multilateral settlement the previously stipulated proportions of the balances on such accounts. The agency would determine the net position of each member taking into consideration the balance on dollar payments and that resulting from the multilateral compensation of parts of bilateral balances. If a country should have a negative or unfavorable balance in its dollar transactions, the agency would grant it automatically a dollar credit equivalent to the excess disbursement as far as permitted by the credit margin of the country. Should a positive balance result, the country would credit the agency with dollars equivalent to the resulting net balance, but not more than the amount of credit margin granted by that country. Net balances resulting from multilateral compensation of bilateral accounts would be incorporated into the system through debits and credits to the swing credit margins.

As may be seen, the *a posteriori* credit system takes

into consideration the fact that convertible currency countries generally carry out their exchange operations through
commercial banks and it would *only require such countries
to lend their positive balance within a predetermined margin and multilaterally.* That positive balance would be com-
puted by the central agency on the basis of data supplied by
the country itself. The availability of this credit would help
prevent a reduction of imports from the zone by deficit
countries in the system; moreover, it would encourage
countries with a positive or favorable balance toward the
rest of the members to increase their purchases in the free-
trade area.

The International Monetary Fund did not react favor-
ably to these proposals. According to the statement made by
a Fund official at the February, 1960, meeting, it objected
not only to the payments system, but also to the idea of a
free-trade area of which an essential element would be multilateral payments arrangements requiring strict adherence
to the principle of reciprocity of tariff and other concessions.
The Fund's main criticism of the payments system, apart
from its skepticism regarding the likelihood of Latin American countries granting each other reciprocal credits, lay in
the automaticity of the credits and the danger that these
might contribute to inflation in a deficit country since the
latter would find it difficult to reduce its debit balance.
Furthermore, the Fund feared that such a country would
abuse the system by diverting toward the free-trade area
purchases which otherwise it would have to pay in convertible currencies outside the area. All this would lead, the
Fund believed, to an impasse in the payments system, when
credit margins would have been exhausted without any possibility of changing the short-term net positions of the
different countries. Therefore, the Fund proposed the adoption of a multilateral compensation system based on balances
freely convertible into any currency.

No agreement could be reached beyond further study of the problem at future meetings. It appears that neither the ECLA proposals nor the Fund's suggestions were acceptable. A new solution must be found by the Executive Committee of the Latin American Free Trade Association established by the Montevideo Treaty, with the technical coöperation and advice of the ECLA Secretariat, the Inter-American ECOSOC and the International Monetary Fund.

It is too early to formulate clear judgment on the whole problem, except to note the gradual evolution from a concept of transferable bilateral balances to the possibility of a system of reciprocal credits—whether or not it may be called a "payments union." This system would accompany the liberalization of trade in the free-trade area and would admit the "coexistence" of transactions in convertible currencies and transactions through bilateral compensation accounts, both of which would operate by means of periodic multilateral settlements through a central agency. Under any system of credits, the establishment of a central agency capable of carrying out these functions is considered "indispensable." [6]

---

[6] ECLA, *The Reciprocal Credits System for the Free-Trade Area* (Working Paper No. 2), January 28, 1960 (reproduced in ECLA document E/CN.12/569 cited in footnote 5).

CHAPTER 7

CENTRAL AMERICA

THE CENTRAL AMERICAN REPUBLICS—Costa Rica, El Salvador, Guatemala, Honduras, and Nicaragua—began their independence as a confederation and remained so until 1838, when they separated. Since that time, they have made several attempts to form a full or partial union, either both political and economic, or only economic, of their five territories. Apart from this historical kinship, economically there is even stronger justification for a Central American common market than for the more general Latin American one. The five countries together have an area barely in excess of 170,000 square miles and their combined population is just over nine and a half million; in comparison, the State of California is only 9 per cent smaller in size and is two-thirds larger in population. The future growth of

Central America's foreign trade, like that of the rest of Latin America, faces inhibiting factors; in addition, trade is subject to sharp short-term fluctuations and is dependent essentially on four products: coffee, cotton, cacao, and bananas, which represent 90 per cent of total exports. Separate industrialization of each country would be very restricted and unequal. Moreover, there is some complementarity in population and economic resources between El Salvador and the other four countries. This has already made possible a relatively substantial amount of reciprocal trade in agricultural products and manufactured consumer goods. However, internal Central American trade has not gone beyond 3 to 4 per cent of the total imports from the region, and about 60 per cent of this trade has been carried out by El Salvador.

This country, following an earlier not very successful attempt, in 1951 embarked on a policy of signing bilateral free-trade treaties with its neighboring countries. Although narrow in scope, such arrangements opened the way to further increases in trade. El Salvador's broad trade treaty of 1917 with Honduras was replaced by an agreement in the new pattern. Only for Nicaragua were special provisions made for possible exchange restrictions; with the others free convertibility in payments was implicit.

Also in 1951, the five countries entered a completely new phase when, with the support of ECLA, they established a program for the economic integration of Central America. At the same time, with the help of other organizations, these countries started to coöperate in political and cultural fields and created the Organization of Central American States. The resolution proposed by the Central American delegations and adopted by ECLA in June, 1951, expressed the interest of the region in "the development of agricultural and industrial production and of transport systems in their respective countries so as to promote the integration of their economies and the expansion of markets by the exchange of their products, the co-ordination of their development programs and the establishment of enterprises in which all or some of these countries have an interest." For this purpose, the ECLA Secretariat was to initiate a number of studies and a committee of ECLA was to be set up as a coördinating agency composed of the ministers of economy of the Central American countries.[1]

As may be seen, the resolution was very broad in scope and was directed toward achieving full integration. The Committee, which was designated the Central American Economic Co-operation Committee, was established in 1952 and, aided by various specialized subcommittees and other bodies, has up to now directed the integration program. Panama was invited to participate and has, in fact, collaborated in specific matters, although it has not formally adhered to the program. In 1959 Panama requested its incorporation, subject to some studies to be made in order to determine the commitments it would have to undertake.[2]

For the present purposes, the various aspects of co-ordination of economic development in Central America in which the advice of ECLA and the help of the technical-assistance programs of the United Nations have played a large role will not be dealt with. Among these topics are: maritime and highway transport; electric energy; tariff nomenclature; customs legislation; weights and measures; housing; statistics; population studies; social policy; taxation; development financing; technological research; public administration; agricultural, forestry and fisheries development, and others. This chapter will consider mainly the measures taken toward the establishment of a common

---

[1] Resolution 9 (IV), June 16, 1951.

[2] See resolution 80 (CCE), September 1, 1951. ECLA, *Report of the Central American Economic Co-operation Committee,* Doc. E/CN.12/533.

market and the coördination of industrial development.

From the beginning, the Central American Economic Co-operation Committee sought a multilateral formula to promote free trade in the region, to provide this trade with industrial content, and stimulate rational industrialization which would avoid duplications that could not be justified even by the aggregate market of the five countries. After a series of Secretariat studies and reports carried out between 1953 and 1956, the Committee, at the suggestion of an *ad hoc* commission of governmental representatives, considered in 1957 a first draft of a multilateral free-trade treaty and a draft of a regime or system for Central American industrial integration. In 1958 this led to a recommendation that the Central American governments sign the respective agreements, which were the Multilateral Treaty on Free Trade and Central American Integration and the Agreement on the Régime for Central American Integration Industries. Both were signed in Tegucigalpa on June 10, 1958, and were subsequently ratified by the legislatures of the five countries, except Costa Rica. The free-trade treaty went into effect upon the deposit of the third ratification.[8]

Under these agreements, the Central American common market was thought of as a free-trade area which in ten years was to be perfected with a view to creating a customs union. At the same time, the establishment and expansion of industries requiring access to the entire Central American market was to be promoted in a coördinated fashion.

The Multilateral Treaty established an initial schedule of commodities on which all duties and charges, except for specified quantitative restrictions, would be immediately abolished. The contracting states also undertook to equal-

---

[8] For the text of the treaties see ECLA, *Report of the Central American Economic Co-operation Committee*, May, 1959, Doc. E/CN.12/492.

ize the tariffs imposed by them with respect to other than Central American countries on products included in the free-trade schedule and those that might be added, as well as on their principal raw materials and the necessary containers.

Under the treaty and in order to provide the greatest possible flexibility to the creation of the common market, special temporary arrangements may be negotiated by which progressive duty reductions would be granted for products not initially listed in the free-trade schedule of commodities, or for products which were to remain subject to quantitative restrictions. Special arrangements may also be negotiated for free trade in specified products between less than the full number of contracting states, provided progressive duty reductions were granted to the remaining country or countries, with the ultimate aim of incorporating such products into the free-trade schedule. The treaty was to be administered through a Central American Trade Commission.

The Agreement on the Régime for Central American Integration Industries was to be applicable to industries defined as those composed of one or more plants in which minimum capacity would require access to the whole Central American market to ensure operation under reasonably economic and competitive conditions. A Central American Industrial Integration Commission was to recommend to the governments the signature of additional protocols concerning those industries that would qualify as "integration industries." Such additional agreements might stipulate, *inter alia,* in which country or countries the plants would be situated, their minimum capacity, the necessary industrial standards, the conditions under which more plants might be admitted to the regime, the regulations that might be advisable for the participation of Central American capital in the corresponding enterprises, and other requirements. Under the agreement, the products of plants covered by the regime were to benefit from free trade; while products of plants not covered by the regime would only benefit from successive annual duty reductions of 10 per cent until the tenth year when they would also enjoy the full benefits of free trade. It was implicitly recognized, therefore, that the application of the free-trade regime of the Multilateral Treaty to certain products of new and important industries would be subject to agreement among the contracting states under the terms of the industrial integration arrangement. In this way, the basis was established for coördinating industrial development by joint agreement whenever the common market would be an essential condition for such development. Provisions were made to promote an equitable geographic distribution of new industrial plants in those branches of industry, so that the principle of industrial reciprocity that underlies the Central American integration program was given practical meaning. However, this industrial agreement did not go into force because it was not ratified by Costa Rica.

Meanwhile, new events have taken place. In September, 1959, the five countries signed the Agreement on the Equalization of Import Duties and Charges, by which they undertook to adopt immediately a single tariff for a specified schedule of commodities and to equalize gradually the tariffs for items listed in another schedule. Once the customs duties on the latter group became equal in the five countries, these products would enjoy completely free trade within a period of five years and, in any case, not later than the ten years provided for in the Multilateral Treaty. The purpose of this agreement was to prepare the ground for a single Central American customs tariff (for which, moreover, a customs nomenclature had been worked out since 1955), thus facilitating the creation of the common market stipulated in the Multilateral Free Trade Treaty.[4] As the initial schedule of free commodities in the latter was rather limited, the contracting states later engaged to sign a protocol to the Agreement on the Equalization of Import Duties and Charges which would permit them to grant each other an immediate tariff preference of 20 per cent for any product not yet transferred to the free-trade schedule.

The position of the Central American proposals toward the provisions of GATT, of which Nicaragua is a contracting party, is not as clear as was the position of the Latin American free-trade area. In 1956, on the basis of an early draft proposal that has since been modified, Nicaragua announced its decision to conclude an agreement leading to the formation of a Central American free-trade area in accordance with Article XXIV of GATT. It was granted the right to benefit from the provisions of this article with the understanding that a definite plan would be drawn up for the formation of a free-trade area within ten years. The resolution adopted by GATT[5] required that Nicaragua should submit that plan to the contracting parties to the General Agreement before September 1, 1960, and it stated that the situation should be subject to review a year later. The recent agreement on tariff equalization and particularly the protocol establishing a 20 per cent Central American preferential tariff would be presumably part of that plan. Although the 20 per cent preference was considered an interim measure to be taken while the free-trade schedules were expanded, it would have to be reconciled with the spirit of the GATT resolution.

---

[4] The agreement establishes for each duty a common equivalent in dollars. It also contains provisions for modification of the duty level in case of a change in the parity of a national currency toward the United States dollar.

[5] GATT, *Basic Instruments and Selected Documents, 5th supplement,* Geneva, 1957, pp. 29–30.

However, the situation in Central America become complicated when in February, 1960, El Salvador, Guatemala, and Honduras signed a triangular agreement apparently not coördinated with the provisions of the Tegucigalpa treaties in which Costa Rica and Nicaragua had taken part. The first three countries signed a treaty of economic association[6] by which they set up a free-trade area that, in five years and provided import duties were first equalized (under the terms of the Central American agreement adhered to by the five countries), would become a customs union with common customs administration, equitable distribution of customs duties, and free movement of any kind of product no matter what its country of origin (that is, including imported products). During the interim stage when the union would function as a free-trade area, imports of products originating in any of the three countries would be exempt from any duty or charge from the date the treaty went into force. Exceptions would be listed in a schedule specifying more favorable treatment for Honduran products as well as gradual duty reductions and quantitative restrictions on foodstuffs, raw materials, and manufactures in which present levels of production might be affected unfavorably by free trade. The system adopted under this triangular treaty was, therefore, unlike that established under the five-country Multilateral Treaty according to which free trade was to be applied only to an initial schedule that would later be expanded by negotiations, provided that the tariffs imposed on the goods of outside countries were equalized at the same time. The Treaty of Economic Association of the three countries went, of course, further toward the creation of a classical customs union.[7]

---

[6] See Centro de Estudios Monetarios Latinoamericanos, *Suplemento al Boletín Quincenal*, March, 1960, pp. 60–63.

[7] If its purpose had been only to establish a temporary regime among the three countries but within the framework of the Multi-

Another important difference between the three-country and the five-country common-market arrangements was that under the latter free trade was related to the idea of a coördinated industrial development to be carried out through the Agreement on Integration Industries in those branches that would be recommended in due time. Instead, the three-country treaty assumed implicitly that industrial development would continue to take place freely without any requirement concerning the coördination of proposals, geographic location of plants, industrial standards, origin of capital resources, and so on. In this respect, the Treaty of Association, by failing to harmonize all economic measures taken by the three countries and to provide greater political and administrative collaboration, might not ensure the balanced economic development that underlies the whole economic integration program, proclaimed and kept alive since 1951 by the original five countries—and now Panama.

The Treaty of Economic Association also included provisions for setting up a Development and Assistance Fund. The functions of the latter were those of a development and loan agency for the carrying out of basic projects—highways and others—and for the establishment or expansion of agricultural and industrial enterprises, especially with a view to offsetting any maladjustments that might arise from the formation of the common market of the three countries. Under the treaty, the statutes of the Fund were to be drafted and signed before June 6, 1960. However, meanwhile, the Economic Co-operation Committee of the five countries, which since 1953 had been dealing with various financial and fiscal aspects of economic integration, recommended in September, 1959, the drafting of a proposal for the creation of a Central American financial agency to promote inte-

lateral Free-Trade Treaty signed by the five countries in 1958, presumably it would have been sufficient to base it on the provisions contained in the latter, which have already been described.

grated economic development "with due regard to the necessity of assigning special priority to the less developed parts of the area." [8]

Despite the provision in the Treaty of Economic Association of El Salvador, Guatemala, and Honduras to the effect that "in accordance with the spirit of Central American solidarity that has inspired the signing of this agreement" the contracting parties were to invite the other Central American countries to participate in the association, it seemed difficult to reconcile the two concepts of a Central American common market. Given the existence at that time of several multilateral treaties relating to the free trade and integration of the region, besides two agreements on highway transportation and at least seven bilateral free-trade treaties; and in the light of competing proposals for the establishment of a Central American development agency and other matters, the Central American program could go no further without a general reappraisal of its aims and methods and a readjustment of all its different factors.

At the end of April, 1960, an extraordinary meeting of the Economic Co-operation Committee was convened for discussion of this problem by the five countries. The ECLA Secretariat was requested to prepare a draft for a Central American agreement on "accelerated economic integration." In the opinion of four of the countries—Costa Rica had expressed reservations—this new draft was to be understood as a general regime of immediate free trade, with the exception of products which might be brought under interim provisions and with the exception also of commodities which, in the terms of the agreement to be signed, would be designated as products of "industrial integration plants." It was foreseen that the common market would be estab-

---

[8] Resolution 84 (CCE), paragraph 4, September 1, 1959. ECLA, *Report of the Central American Economic Co-operation Committee*, Doc. E/CN.12/533.

lished within five years and that a single customs tariff
would be adopted, together with a system of common incentives for industrial development and "the necessary measures to achieve uniform social charges." Furthermore, the
formation of a Central American Development Financing
Agency would be considered and provisions made to permit
any country which did not sign the new agreement to adhere later.[9]

The new negotiations led to the signing in Managua
in December, 1960, of the General Treaty of Central American Economic Integration, of a protocol to the Agreement
on Equalization of Import Duties and Charges, and of the
Basic Statutes for the Central American Economic Integration Bank. Costa Rica did not sign any of these agreements
and, since it has not ratified the previous multilateral arrangements, it is in fact now excluded from the Central
American integration program.

The General Treaty signed by the four remaining
countries has now gone into force. It stipulates a five-year
time limit for the creation of a common market and binds
the contracting parties to the setting up of a customs union
with a single external tariff. This treaty adopts the system
underlying the three-country Treaty of Association that has
been mentioned. It establishes free trade immediately for
all products originating in the territories of the signatory
countries, except for those products, specified in annexes to
the agreement, which will be brought under special interim
arrangements until they may become totally free. Therefore, the treaty includes long and complicated lists of products for which customs treatment by pairs of countries will
be progressively modified. Some products will enter into
free trade in two years, others in three, in four, during the

---

[9] Resolution 101 (CCE), April 28, 1960. See ECLA, *Report
of the Second Extraordinary Meeting of the Central American Economic Co-operation Committee*, Doc. E/CN.12/552.

five years envisaged, or never. Moreover, many products will also be subject to export controls or various conditions such as the provisions of other treaties or of future arrangements for industrial, agricultural, and commercial coördination. The treaty also assumes the provisions of the Central American industrial integration regime that had been signed earlier by the five countries but that never went into force because of Costa Rica's failure to ratify. Through this means, the latter regime was adopted by the four countries and is expected to be effectively applied soon. The four signatory countries decided to set up a Central American Economic Council, an Executive Council of the Treaty, and a permanent secretariat. The functions of these bodies will also cover the other multilateral treaties subscribed to, except for the agreement establishing the Economic Integration Bank which has its own executive and administrative organs.

The bank, which was inaugurated in May, 1961, started with a capital of sixteen million dollars and has received the support of the Inter-American Development Bank. Its principal function will be to consider projects which may promote the economic integration and general economic improvement of the region. These projects may relate to basic social overhead or to certain agricultural or industrial activities. The bank will not undertake to finance projects of purely local interest. Apparently, special attention will be given to proposals that will tend to reduce the economic differences between the four countries. Furthermore it is understood that the creation of this agency fulfills the purposes of the earlier three-country treaty of association to create a development and assistance fund.

The Central American Bank may perhaps contribute to an effective promotion of integration of the region, since financial incentives usually overcome much of the resistance to the acceptance of free trade; but it remains to be seen how soon the other agreements will be implemented. Much work has been done in the past few months to prepare the Central American uniform import tariff. Even if this important requirement is met, there are still many other problems to solve and, above all, it does not appear that the governments are firmly committed to apply an effective economic integration policy. In Central America, many general political and economic problems necessarily take precedence over economic integration. The progress of the program has been slow; since its initiation almost nine years ago it has yielded few positive results. In effect, three concepts of integration coexist in Central America: one, of broad Central American scope, includes, at least theoretically, the five countries; a second one, expressed through the bilateral treaties and the three-country agreement, does not assume that development will necessarily be coördinated by the countries; and a third, now in force, envisages a partly planned integration of the four countries with the possibility of Costa Rica adhering to the system when it decides to do so.

At different times, such as during the Economic Conference of Buenos Aires in 1957 and during the eighth and ninth sessions of ECLA in 1959 and 1961, the Central American countries have claimed for themselves the right to be an exception to the proposals for a more general Latin American common market, in order to consolidate first their own regional market and later to enter the Latin American free-trade area as a unit. It would not be advisable to permit the Central American customs union and the Latin American free-trade area to function as watertight compartments and undoubtedly it will be necessary to study at an early date how the two groups can become associated.

Much of the experience gained in Central America is useful to the broader problems of Latin American coöperation. For example, the studies effected and the methods worked out for the treatment of common problems of transportation, housing, industrial development, electric energy, agricultural coördination, statistics, and others; especially studies relating to tariff nomenclature, measurement of the incidence of import duties, procedures for equalizing customs duties, preparation of a uniform customs tariff, and comparative studies of systems of tax exemptions for industrial promotion. There are also valuable lessons to be drawn from the coöperation in technological research, productivity studies and public administration training. Furthermore, the need to consider the economic development of a region as a whole has become an accepted idea. All these are positive aspects of the collaboration between the countries and of the technical assistance and advice given by the international organizations participating in the program.[10]

[10] There are numerous documents concerning the Central American integration program and its various specialized aspects. For an over-all view, see the following: ECLA, *La integración económica de Centroamérica: su evolución y perspectivas* (United Nations Publication, 1956. II.G.4; available only in Spanish); ECLA, "Central American Economic Integration Programme: Evaluation and Prospects," *Economic Bulletin for Latin America*, Vol. IV, No. 2, Santiago, Chile, October, 1959, pp. 34–39; and the annual reports of the Central American Economic Co-operation Committee, ECLA, from 1952 to date (the most recent, Doc. E/CN.12/552, refers to the seventh meeting held in December, 1960).

PART THREE

THE CURRENT SITUATION

CHAPTER 8

SOME PROBLEMS OF

FREE TRADE AND INTEGRATION

THE CONCEPT OF FREE TRADE in Latin America and the steps taken toward trade liberalization and economic integration have evolved in agreements, especially the Montevideo Treaty, which are proof of the maturity of contemporary Latin American thought on important aspects of future economic development. However, these agreements are merely legal instruments which cannot, alone, solve the problems of free trade. They can only establish general rules to guide the participating countries in the formulation of both their national and joint policies toward a common market. Many common-market problems must be solved in the coming years if free trade is to be a significant factor in the economic and social development of Latin America.

Perhaps the most important of these problems is to

increase membership in the free-trade area set up by the
Montevideo Treaty. Although geographic expansion of the
zone will complicate the implementation and operation of
the agreement, the remaining Latin American countries, or
at least those strongest economically and most highly developed, ought to be incorporated. Such expansion would not
only broaden the prospects of heavy industry and many
other related activities; it would go a considerable way
toward diversifying the markets of the relatively less developed countries and would, therefore, facilitate their industrial growth. In providing for the incorporation of other
countries, the Montevideo Treaty imposes a greater readjustment upon those countries which delay accession too
long, for they are required to match the extent of the concessions already reached by the original members. The most
appropriate time for the incorporation of new members
would be during the first two years of the treaty or, at the
latest, before the drawing up of the first three-year period
of the common schedule which will bring 25 per cent of
the value of reciprocal trade under the free-trade regime.[1]

As for those Latin American countries which have considered their overvalued currency to hamper their entry
into the common market, it is perhaps better to view the
problem as one of finding a purchasing-power parity with
reference to which tariff comparisons and concessions can
be made on products of excessively protected industries.
Care should be taken, however, to permit maximum tariff
reduction on products of industries in which high productivity may counteract the apparent effect of overvaluation.
With the passage of time, the accession of this type of country will become increasingly difficult especially if it does

---

[1] The present trade *between* the member countries of the area
represents approximately one-half of all intra-Latin American
trade, which leaves an appreciable margin of trade to be incorporated, even without taking into account its future increase.

not take part in the initial negotiations for industrial or agricultural arrangements of complementation and specialization.

The case of the Central American countries presents a special aspect of the question of expanding the free-trade area. It has been assumed that these countries would enter as a unit with a single tariff, or at least one that is being unified at the same time that trade is liberalized within the region. Their economic integration program is presently at an undefined stage which may isolate them from the Latin American free-trade area; this would be detrimental to some industries that can be developed in Central America. In general, obligations contracted before the Montevideo Treaty, including subregional associations like the Central American, border trade and other agreements, will remain unaltered; although it may be expected that efforts will be made to harmonize or resolve important inconsistencies.

As has been suggested, the expansion of the free-trade area is closely related to one of the fundamental concerns implicit in any scheme of economic association or union: the relative advantages which one member of the zone may gain at the expense of the other members. Historical instances in which a common market produces an apparent "polarization" of industrial activity have been cited and the fear has been expressed that this will happen in Latin America; that is to say, that existing inequalities in the level of development of the more advanced as compared with the less advanced countries will be accentuated.[2] This fear could influence some countries against entering the common market. Nevertheless, they might be still worse off if they did not enter. Even in the best of circumstances, if such a country should find a new item for export to world markets which would permit it to disregard the possibilities of the

---

[2] Sidney S. Dell, *Problemas de un mercado común en América Latina*, pp. 42–54.

Latin American market and to do without the advantages of
solidarity, the limited size of its domestic market would
never support an adequate and efficient industrial development; and this would be especially important if that country
had a high present or potential population density. The
problem is, rather, to implement effectively the provisions
of the Montevideo Treaty for favored treatment—perhaps
on a long-term basis—of the less developed countries; just
as the improvement of a backward area within any country
becomes the responsibility of the nation as a whole. Polarization is not unavoidable, especially if free trade is not
suddenly and absolutely established but is expanded in a
gradual and controlled fashion and is, to some extent, directed and planned. Naturally, it is not possible to go to
the extreme of creating a large-scale heavy industry in each
Latin American country. However, the opportunities for
greater geographic diversification and adequate specialization will not be so limited as to deprive any country of the
concrete benefits resulting from the creation of the common
market.

The preceding topics are related to the coördination
of industrial and agricultural development, an idea that is
contained in the common-market proposals and in the general provisions of the Montevideo Treaty. The purpose of
this coördination would be to avoid duplication and to
secure adequate complementarity and specialization, which
would, in turn, permit the setting up of plants with low
operating costs and would contribute to regional equi-
librium. In general, it would mean a saving of resources. In
an ideal situation, where each country in the free-trade area
had an integrated development program, it would also be
possible to draw up over-all programs establishing joint policies for the promotion of at least the principal industrial,
extractive, and agricultural activities. Latin American conditions will inevitably impose other, more modest, methods;

specific branches of industry and agriculture will probably be coördinated progressively and often partially, on a voluntary basis, and depending on individual circumstances. As the products of these sectors come under free trade, there will undoubtedly be an increasing interest in coördination.

The coördination of industrial growth does not imply either a prejudice in favor of state control of economic activities or restrictions on the freedom of action of private enterprise; nor should it mean the transformation of competition into private cartels or monopolies. The essential requirement is that projections be made for the basic sectors of production of capital goods, intermediate products, and some durable consumer goods—especially those for which demand tends to increase more rapidly; and that they indicate over-all needs, how best to meet them, and with what financial resources. Taking into account all projections, the relative advantages of various locations and the possibilities for complementary development could be determined for each branch or sector, and general agreements could be worked out between governments. Although private enterprise would be at liberty to make specific plans, naturally where industry is partly owned by the state, public and private interests would have to be reconciled.

The way has been pointed by studies made in Latin America in recent years on the situation and prospects of industrial sectors such as steel, pulp and paper, iron and steel manufactures, basic chemicals and, to a lesser extent, the manufacture of automobiles, railroad cars, and other equipment. But this type of work will have to be intensified and extended to many other sectors. At the same time, it is necessary to go ahead with important programs to standardize specifications and quality, in addition to programs of productivity and technological research.

Coördination should be easier to achieve, at least theoretically, in agricultural activities, which are subject to price policies and other forms of regulation in almost all countries. It should be possible to estimate the short-term outlook for supply and demand in food products and some agricultural raw materials and, through consultative machinery, to foresee the short-term deficits and surpluses of member countries of the free-trade area. In this way and, of course, according to price, credit, currency of payment, and other factors, the opportunities for intraregional trade would be used before resorting to imports from outside Latin America. In addition to this short-term aspect of coördination, there is the long-term consideration of productivity and alternative uses of resources in order to decide in which countries to locate future agricultural developments and some of the related processing and manufacturing industries. As in the basic industrial sectors, the joint study of prospects and possibilities might lead to general agreements between governments which would result in a considerable expansion of intraregional trade. In Latin America, the coördination of agriculture would benefit those countries which are relatively less developed but especially suited for agricultural production and it would offset any disadvantage they might fear from a concentrated industrialization of other countries of the zone.

The deficiencies and difficulties of transportation will make necessary close coöperation between members of the free-trade area. More important than the lack of means of transportation are the inadequacy and high operational cost of many ports and the absence of regular service on some routes. Fortunately, the existence of several South American shipping companies demonstrates that it is not impossible to furnish efficient service. Rather than to create special services for Latin American trade, the existing ones should be adapted and developed. The entry of more countries into the free-trade area would obviously be to the advantage of transportation, as it would signify an increased volume of cargo and the possible contribution of national shipping services.

Among the problems that would probably require immediate attention in the free-trade area are many related to the implementation of the provisions for the elimination of duties, charges, and other restrictions and for the achievement of uniformity in measures that concern outside countries. The negotiations for the annual 8 per cent reduction in the weighted average of each country's tariff will inevitably be complex, even as to the methods of calculation provided by the treaty. Moreover, since a reduction will be sought in restrictions which are equivalent to tariffs—such as quantitative restrictions, prior deposits in domestic currency for foreign-exchange allocations, and the like—it will be necessary to work out a method for equating tariffs with other restrictions. Still another problem, of even greater complexity, originates in the disparity between the customs tariffs of the member countries of the zone toward the rest of the world. It is not simply a question of comparing the over-all incidence of taxes imposed by each country on its total imports, but rather of comparing tariff rates, product by product, using a standard method and taking into account the effect of quantitative restrictions as well as that of import duties. Such comparisons will be required as long as significant discrepancies exist, because a country which adopts lower external tariffs would, in effect, be granting other member countries a smaller margin of preference. A low import tariff on raw materials or the unassembled part of a product could by itself attract enterprises to one country to the detriment of the others; or it might stimulate activities in which the value added by domestic manufacture would be small. All this is related to the equally intricate problem of determining the origin of commodities, that is, whether they are articles produced in the free-trade area. Eventually, external tariffs will have to be reconciled on the basis of individual products, in order to eliminate at least the most conspicuous discrepancies. Of course, as the common market approaches realization, the adoption of a uniform tariff must be studied.

Implicit in these measures is the gradual development of joint foreign-trade policies which would govern relations with GATT, bilateral treaties with countries outside the area, and general negotiations, such as those on basic products. But since the commercial and monetary aspects of foreign trade are inseparable, greater coöperation on external monetary policy will also be demanded of member countries. It is true that this policy now derives from each country's foreign economic relations as a whole, which are only influenced by the proportionately small intraregional trade to the extent that past bilateral agreements may have current unfavorable repercussions. However, the future importance of the free-trade area will make each country more aware of the others' decisions on foreign monetary policy, especially as they move toward systems of full and effective monetary convertibility. Since a devaluation is equivalent to a temporary restriction on imports, a member of the free-trade area could claim some compensation if its trade prospects in a country were significantly altered by that member's devaluation. On the other hand, a country in which costs had risen by inflation might, through devaluation, restore its industries to a competitive position in the zone. At the present time, monetary stabilization programs have been adopted or drawn up by all countries of the free-trade area; but there is no guarantee that these programs will not be affected by a recession in the international markets or by the inflationary bias of the process of development in some countries.

The problem of the multilateralization of bilateral balances, discussed in chapter 6, is still under study by the members of the free-trade area. Some countries prefer to trade on the basis of dollars or, at least, of convertible bilateral balances. Others, enjoying less favorable conditions, consider it necessary to maintain bilateral accounts and to seek multilateral compensation of the resulting balances. More general proposals have been presented for the adoption of a mixed system in which some countries would use dollars and others would keep bilateral accounts which would be settled, in part, multilaterally; this system would operate together with a mechanism for reciprocal credits which would also be multilateralized through a central agency. The International Monetary Fund opposes these ideas partly because it judges full convertibility to be so close at hand that the creation of a mechanism for compensation is superfluous. Nevertheless, inconvertibility exists in fact now and may recur at any moment, so that the problem of adopting a system of reciprocal credits, in whatever currency, persists. Such a system would facilitate the maintenance of new trade flows and their steady expansion. As happens everywhere, the development of new types of trade in machinery and other equipment must be financed by medium and long-term credit. A multilateral credit system would be preferable to a series of bilateral agreements. In addition, there should be opportunities to rediscount a part of the balances outside of the free-trade area. A greater volume of trade implies an increase in inventories, and these cannot usually be financed without credit. The multilateralization of already existing bilateral situations will probably be more important in the early stages of the implementation of the Montevideo Treaty; but as the volume of trade in manufactured goods expands, the development of a credit system will become increasingly urgent.

The free-trade area will also benefit from coöperation and coördination in the field of foreign financing. Various sources have expressed the fear that the Latin American common market may offer excessive advantages to private foreign investment at the expense of national capital. Putting aside the question of how much foreign capital the free-trade area might attract—an amount that still cannot be estimated—there is still the problem of the advantages to be gained for its new industries by one country over the others by fiscal or other legislation which may be less restrictive or more favorable to foreign capital. Such differences in treatment and their implications are already being studied. As for other ways of financing development with foreign resources, it is evident that international banking organizations and other agencies will be more likely to support projects relating to the common market if they are presented jointly by the member countries of the free zone. The Inter-American Development Bank will undoubtedly tend to give special attention to requests which strengthen the objectives of free trade, even though it will not exclude from consideration the individual projects of any member.

Any association creates common interests and any economic association creates common economic interests. As in Europe, the Latin American free-trade area and, ultimately, the common market, will only progress if the member countries are capable of submitting their national interests—which should never be neglected—to the interests of the region as a whole; and to do this by negotiation and mutual confidence, because eventually the interests of the region will coincide with the interests of the individual countries.

Latin America faces not merely a trade aspect of its economic life but the entire pattern of a possible joint economic development. Latin American integration is less a defense than a necessity; the alternative to union is to remain at low standards of living. The proposals undeniably contain defensive features designed to meet the unfavorable effects which developments such as the participation of African territories in the European common market will have on the outlook for many traditional Latin American exports. However, it is not an aggressive plan; for their future growth, the Latin American countries must make use of all the equipment and technique that their available monetary or financial resources can acquire from the rest of the world. In the final analysis, a common market in Latin America is a requisite for economic growth and, at the same time, a safeguard for the trade and evolution of the industrial countries in the rest of the world.

POSTSCRIPT

On June 1, 1961, the Montevideo Treaty entered into force for the original seven signatory countries: Argentina, Brazil, Chile, Mexico, Paraguay, Peru, and Uruguay. The time limit granted to Bolivia for its accession as a relatively less developed country to the Latin American Free Trade Association was extended; but the government of this country still did not consider itself in a position to assume the obligations of the treaty. On the other hand, Colombia and Ecuador, as the result of new consultative meetings held with Venezuela, announced their intention to adhere to the association and took the necessary measures to do so at an early date. Venezuela preferred to postpone consideration of its possible adherence to the association until a more thorough study could be made of the problems arising from its economic structure and from its high level of dollar costs. In addition to Bolivia and Venezuela, therefore, the following countries are still outside the Latin American free trade area: Cuba, Haiti, Panama, the Dominican Republic, and the Central American republics (four of which, El Salvador, Guatemala, Honduras, and Nicaragua, are establishing their own common market).

Thus the region is still faced with the problem mentioned at the beginning of chapter 8 as perhaps the most important one: that of its limited geographic extension. However, the rapid and efficient manner in which Ecuador and Colombia, together with Venezuela, examined their economic relations with the member countries of the zone has been encouraging. They discussed several alternatives and were able to reach decisions which, although different for each country, were based on common interests born partly of the old Grancolombian association.[1] The entry of additional countries will undoubtedly benefit both the new members and the zone as a whole, since it will multiply the possibilities of expanding industrial development. It is to be hoped that Venezuela and the other countries, with the help of experts of the Association's Standing Executive Committee and of ECLA, will make an effort to find a solution which will furnish the safeguards necessary for their adherence to the association.

During the time between the signature of the Montevideo Treaty at the beginning of 1960 and its recent entry into force, much study was given to specific problems relating to the provisions of the treaty and to the adjustment of tariff and trade policies and practices of the member countries. One of the principal questions was the treaty's position toward GATT. Extended and detailed consultations were carried out between the GATT Secretariat and the Montevideo Provisional Committee; and the parties of

---

[1] Of great interest is a document entitled *Consultations on Commercial Policy: Report on the Third Series of Meetings Held between Colombia, Ecuador and Venezuela* (Quito, December 7–10, 1960), issued by ECLA in 1961 and containing several papers prepared by the ECLA Secretariat (Doc. E/CN.12/555).

the former took the matter under consideration at the seventeenth session of GATT in November, 1960. On recommendations from a working group, the parties concluded that although there remained legal and practical doubts which could only be resolved in the light of the application of the treaty, this would not prevent the parties to the Montevideo Treaty that were also parties to GATT from proceeding to establish the Latin American free-trade area. This decision is significant mainly because it demonstrates that the more important countries in world trade are generally in agreement with the formation of the free-trade area and with the projected development of Latin America as a regional group in harmony with the broader objectives of expanding world trade to which almost every country is committed.

The preparations to negotiate the first annual reduction of 8 per cent of the weighted average of the import tariffs of members of the area took several months in each country, because of the need to study the markets and their possibilities, to gather data on import duties, quotas and other restrictions, and to consult the opinion of private industrial and agricultural groups. In addition to the official exchange of information, representatives of both public and private industries of the signatory countries began a series of visits and surveys to explore specific opportunities for trade and for agreements to coördinate future development. These contacts intensified a trend already apparent toward greater interest in Latin American markets by industrial enterprises which had not exploited their export capacity because of the excessive protection of some of these markets and because of payments difficulties.

In the field of customs-tariffs techniques, the ECLA Secretariat, working closely with the provisional authorities of the Montevideo Treaty, carried out comparative studies

that had never been done before on the tariff levels and
quantitative restrictions existing in Latin American countries, on the conciliation of foreign-trade statistics, and on
transport problems. Various intergovernmental meetings
were held on these topics. FAO, in collaboration with
ECLA, prepared new studies on the possibilities of trade in
agricultural commodities. The third meeting of the ECLA
Trade Committee, held in Santiago, Chile, in May, 1961,
endorsed all this work.

However, the question of multilateral payments compensation was almost abandoned, while all attention was
centered on securing the ratification and entry into force of
the treaty. In spite of the extent to which some South
American countries have progressed toward currency convertibility, there are a number of bilateral arrangements
still in effect that will make trade on the basis of equal
treatment difficult with other member countries of the area.
And the settlement of all balances in convertible currencies
does not yet appear to be possible with countries like Brazil
which have only begun to reorganize their exchange systems and to adjust their financial relations with the rest of
the world.

Chapters 6 and 8 mentioned the need, which has been
stressed in many quarters, of facilitating a larger volume of
trade by means of reciprocal credits to promote trade in new
manufactures, especially machinery and equipment. If suitable credit is not available to these new lines of production,
many of the more dynamic industries of member countries
of the area will not be able to benefit from the potential
of the Latin American markets, since they will compete
under less favorable conditions than some of the European,
North American, or Japanese suppliers. There have been
instances in which a Latin American country, because of a
very short schedule of repayments, has been unable to purchase in the region equipment which competed in quality

and price with foreign equipment.² Some European countries, during the ninth session of ECLA held in May, 1961, opposed the idea that the Latin American countries should conclude arrangements to permit granting each other medium and long-term credits for export. But this attitude seems to be derived from an inadequate grasp of the problem and it is to be hoped that, in accordance with the more general purpose of making the Latin American free-trade area an efficient instrument to accelerate economic development, industrial countries will help solve the credit problem. Meanwhile, the Inter-American Development Bank has taken up its study.

Insistently the question has been raised, in Latin America, in the United States, and in Europe, whether the Montevideo Treaty has a real chance of success. This question takes different forms. One, which would hardly be worth considering if it did not represent, unfortunately, a deep-rooted point of view in influential circles of public opinion, believes that the attempt to create a free trade area and ultimately a common market in Latin America is only one more of those romantic and emotional declarations which so abundantly adorn the history of this region. Because of a lack of understanding of the difficulties that Latin America faces in its economic development, this point of view also finds in the series of safeguards and special conditions provided by the Montevideo Treaty "proof" that the area will be ineffective. Respectable government officials, businessmen, university professors, and economists, inclined to take a negative attitude and to forget both international realities and those of their own countries, predict the failure of the Latin American free-trade area because, according to them,

---

² See ECLA, *The Latin American Movement Towards Multilateral Economic Co-operation*, E/CN.12/567, March, 1961, paragraph 43. See also paragraphs 14 to 16, regarding the general payments situation.

it does not correspond to some theoretical free-trade model of the textbooks or because it permits "too much" state intervention. And so they adopt the classic posture of the ostrich that naïvely tries to protect itself from the strong adverse winds swirling around it—in this case, the irrepressible forces of economic and social development in Latin America.

Then there are the skeptics who are well acquainted with the Latin American situation but stress the resistance that certainly will be put up by many industrial and agricultural interests. Thanks to high tariff and exchange protection, such groups, both large and small, occupy monopolistic positions which they will be reluctant to surrender. Undoubtedly, the free-trade area will have to contend with this opposition; it is also a domestic problem. Many Latin American industrial enterprises, planned badly or designed for larger markets, operate at high costs; they often have inefficient equipment or for various reasons have been unable to modernize; and they may exploit market situations which allow them to maintain high prices. But there is also a number of entirely modern enterprises directed by a new type of entrepreneur who has a dynamic vision of his country's economy. Sooner or later, domestic competition and the progressive growth of the domestic market will compel the adoption of productivity improvements that will make these industries competitive in Latin America and that will enable them also to compete efficiently with outside industries. This process is already taking place in almost every country of the zone. A more or less natural modernization program will be accompanied by an official policy intended to raise productivity, introduce new technology, and persuade entrepreneurs of the advantages of the additional Latin American market. Often the initiative has come from the entrepreneurs themselves. On the other hand, the machinery of the treaty does not provide for sudden and total elimination of customs duties, but only for gradual reductions. The present trend seems to be toward negotiating concessions with regard to a large variety of industrial manufactured products, many of which will enter internal Latin American competition, and not toward limiting concessions to a few purely complementary products.

The foregoing is related to the opinion held by a third group of pessimists who question whether the treaty will lead to a reduction of charges and restrictions only on products which are already traded—in which case, the prospects would be very limited indeed—or whether it will also include commodities which up to now have not, for understandable reasons, been traded between the countries. This opinion has been expressed in various ways but usually appears to be the result of a too literal interpretation of the treaty. It is alleged mainly that the treaty *requires* the liberalization of existing trade, but *does not require* and *only makes possible,* at the discretion of the contracting parties, the reduction of duties, charges, and other restrictions on so-called "new" products.[3] It is stated that the formula provided by the Protocol to the Treaty for calculating weighted averages of duties operates in such a way that by reducing the duty only on products which are already traded a country may fulfill the agreement's requirement of an annual reduction of 8 per cent. These same authors recognize that the governments obviously must not have intended the treaty to have such a narrow application. But even a literal interpretation of the treaty does not really justify their posi-

---

[3] See, for example, Raymond F. Mikesell, "The Movement Toward Regional Trading Groups in Latin America," in *Latin American Issues: Essays and Comments* (ed. Albert O. Hirschman), New York, 1961, especially pp. 135–139; and even ECLA, in an article on the free-trade area in the *Economic Bulletin for Latin America,* Vol. V, No. 1, March, 1960, and, more recently, in *The Latin American Movement Towards Multilateral Economic Co-operation,* paragraph 5.

tion. Article 14 establishes that "in order to ensure the continued expansion and diversification of reciprocal trade, the Contracting Parties shall take steps . . . (b) to include in the National Schedules the largest possible number of products in which trade is carried on among the Contracting Parties; and (c) to add to these Schedules an increasing number of products which are not yet included in reciprocal trade." In other words, no distinction is drawn between products which are already traded and so-called "new" products, either as to sequence or as to purpose. The signatory countries agree to take steps to include the products of both categories in the schedules of commodities that are subject to duty reductions. It is evident that some authors have also misunderstood the formula for calculating the 8 per cent annual reduction of the weighted average; they have assumed that the customs duty on each product is to be weighted with the value of imports of the product originating only in the other countries of the Latin American free-trade area, when the relevant provision makes completely clear that the weighting is to be done with the "total value of imports, *irrespective* of origin" (Title I, paragraph 6, section *b* of the Protocol). By weighting the duties in this way, as many "new" products may be added through negotiation to intrazonal trade as may be desired; therefore, the idea that the treaty is restricted to the liberation of existing trade is entirely unfounded.

Moreover, this controversy seems rather pointless. The Montevideo Treaty was signed in order to make possible a future volume of trade that would ensure the expansion of industrial sectors which are essential to present and future development in Latin America (even if some still do not export anything); otherwise several countries would not have taken part in the negotiations, and much less have committed their national and international policies and the word of their political leaders. A mere examination of the schedule of commodities proposed by each signatory country for the first negotiations now underway to reduce duties and eliminate restrictions demonstrates that at no time did these countries intend the treaty to have a limited and theoretical scope.

There is no doubt that the process of liberalizing internal Latin American trade will be, as already stated, complicated and beset with numerous difficulties. The procedures foreseen in the treaty have seemed to many observers to be slow and cumbersome, perhaps excessively cautious. But the procedure is one thing, and another is the policy that is likely to be carried out. Policies are affected by a number of different factors, among them the critical situation of Latin America's trade with the rest of the world, because of the excess supply of many basic products and the slow increase in their foreign demand. More and more it is recognized that industrialization must be promoted, and the treaty is certainly an instrument which would favor industrial growth, a better utilization of resources, and an adequate planning of the new industries that Latin America needs and is about to create.

Actually, since Latin America still has no experience in the multilateral freeing of trade, predictions would be hazardous; but it is not improbable that after the Montevideo Treaty's first year of application the member countries might find it advisable, as the countries of the European Common market have, to accelerate the formation of the free-trade area by increasing the amount of products incorporated and by shortening the stages of liberalization.

APPENDIXES

APPENDIX A

CHRONOLOGY OF THE COMMON MARKET

BEFORE 1938   Various plans for creating a Latin American customs union or partial unions, without any practical result.

1939–1947   Agreement negotiated by Argentina and Brazil for industrial complementation and free trade (1939). Proposal for River Plate Customs Union (1941). Various bilateral free-trade agreements proposed or actually signed: El Salvador—Guatemala (1941), Haiti—Dominican Republic, Argentina with several Latin American countries. Bilateral payments agreements signed between a number of countries of Latin America.

1940   Agreement drawn up to create the Inter-American Bank which, in addition to its other functions, was to operate as a payments compensation center.

1948–1955   Bilateral treaties of economic union and payments signed between Argentina and several other Latin American countries.

1948   Resolutions adopted by ECLA regarding the study of a Latin American customs union and a payments union. Proposal for a customs union between Colombia, Ecuador, Panama, and Venezuela (Quito Charter). [In Europe, entry into force of customs union between Belgium, Luxemburg, and the Netherlands (Benelux); setting up of the Organization for European Economic Co-operation which comprises sixteen countries; creation of the European Payments Union.][1]

1949   Proposal put forth by Uruguay to establish a regional payments-compensation mechanism. Report by the International Monetary Fund, at the request of ECLA, on the possibility and advisability of establishing a system of multilateral payments compensation. ECLA resolution requesting further studies.

1951   ECLA resolution launching the Central American economic integration program.

1951–1957   Seven bilateral free-trade treaties signed between countries of Central America. [In Europe, *July 1951*: Adoption of OEEC trade-liberalization code.]

1952   First meeting of the Central American Economic Co-operation Committee. [In Europe, establishment of the European Coal and Steel Community.]

1952–1955   Studies by ECLA on intra-Latin American and intra-Central American trade. [*June*,

---

[1] Some important events related to the European Common Market have been inserted in square brackets.

1955: In Italy, Messina Conference; agreement to create a European Common Market.] *September, 1955:* ECLA resolution establishing the Trade Committee.

1956   *August:* Report by two ECLA consultants on the possibility of a regional market. *November:* First meeting of the Trade Committee of ECLA; resolution adopted by GATT on the participation of Nicaragua in a Central American free-trade area.

1957   *January:* Draft agreements on a Central American free-trade and economic integration treaty and on a Central American industrial integration regime. [In Europe, report by a working group on the possible relationship between the European Common Market and the other eleven members of the OEEC; *February:* A committee appointed to prepare a draft agreement on a free trade area. *March:* Signature of the Rome Treaty setting up the European Economic Community (European Common Market) between West Germany, Belgium, France, Italy, Luxemburg, and the Netherlands.] *May:* Standard agreement on bilateral-payments drafted by a working group of eight South American central banks, which also recommends the voluntary multilateral settlement of balances; ECLA resolution supporting Trade Committee work program on the regional market and the possibility of multilateral payments compensation. From *June* onward: Adoption of the standard agreement by Argentina, Bolivia, Chile and Uruguay. *September:* Declaration at the Economic Conference of the Organization of American States on the advisability of a Latin American regional market. [In Europe, during 1957, meetings of experts from Denmark, Finland, Norway, and Sweden to draft proposals for a Nordic common market.]

1958   [*January:* Entry into force of the Rome Treaty on the European Common Market.] *February:* First meeting of the ECLA working group to prepare bases for a Latin American regional market. *June:* Signature of the Tegucigalpa Treaty creating a Central American common market. *July:* United Nations Economic and Social Council resolution on the advisability of a Latin American regional market. *August:* Consultative meeting of experts from Argentina, Brazil, Chile, and Uruguay to consider a program of trade liberalization between those countries and the possibility of a Latin American preferential regime. *September:* Declaration in Washington of the foreign ministers of the American Republics, *inter alia,* on the advisability of accelerating efforts to create "regional markets" in Latin America. *November:* Communication from Brazil and Chile to GATT concerning a possible draft agreement on a Latin American preferential zone; consultations with the GATT Secretariat. *December:* Draft proposal by a working group of central banks for a Latin American system of multilateral compensation of bilateral balances (draft Rio de Janeiro Protocol).

1959   [*January:* Entry into force of first 10 per cent tariff reduction between members of the European Common Market.] *February:* Second meeting of the ECLA working group to make recommendations on the structure and basic principles of a Latin American common market. *April:* Meeting of experts from Argentina, Brazil, Chile, and Uruguay to prepare, with the collaboration of the ECLA Secretariat, a draft for a free-trade zone (Santiago draft) open to adherence by other Latin American countries. Consultative meetings in Caracas of experts from Colombia, Ecuador, and Venezuela on trade policy between the three countries. *May:* Second meeting of the ECLA Trade Committee; resolution on the bases for a Latin American common market and on the convening of a meeting of governmental experts to prepare a preliminary draft treaty; resolution on new studies on payments problems. *May-June:* Consultations of Argentina, Brazil, Chile, and Uruguay with the GATT Secretariat concerning the Santiago draft. *June:* modification of the Santiago draft by governmental experts from Argentina, Bolivia, Brazil, Chile, Paraguay, Peru, and Uruguay (Lima draft); diplomatic conference convened by Uruguay to draw up an official proposal. *September:* Conference in Montevideo of representatives of Argentina, Bolivia, Brazil, Chile, Paraguay, Peru, and Uruguay, together with observers from Mexico and Venezuela, to prepare a draft proposal for a Latin American free-trade area open to adherence by other countries (Montevideo draft); signature in San José, Costa Rica, of a Central American treaty on equalization of customs tariffs and a protocol on tariff preferences. *November:* Communication to GATT by Argentina, Bolivia, Brazil, Chile, Peru, and Uruguay concerning the proposal for a free-trade zone. [Signature of the Stockholm Agreement establishing the European Free Trade Association and creating a free-trade area between Austria, Denmark, Norway, Portugal, Sweden, Switzerland, and the United Kingdom.] *December:* United Nations General Assembly resolution on the

Latin American common market; creation of
the Inter-American Development Bank.

1960   *January:* Meeting in Montevideo of representatives of Latin American central banks to consider the payments problem; ECLA proposals
for a system of multilateral reciprocal credits.
February: Signature of the Treaty of Economic Association by El Salvador, Guatemala,
and Honduras establishing a free-trade area
between the three countries; drafting in
Montevideo by representatives of eight Latin
American governments of the official proposal
for the free-trade area. *February 18: Signature
of the Montevideo Treaty creating a free-trade
area between Argentina, Brazil, Chile, Mexico,
Paraguay, Peru, and Uruguay and establishing
the Latin American Free-Trade Association;*
Bolivia's adherence postponed. *April:* Setting
up in Montevideo of the Provisional Committee of the Latin American Free-Trade Association. [*May:* Decision by the European Economic Community to accelerate the formation
of the European Common Market.] *May-De-
cember:* Consultations begun between the Provisional Committee and the GATT Secretariat;
preparation and publication by signatory countries of schedules of products on which they
will request reduction or elimination of duties
and restrictions in the Latin American Free-
Trade Association; work on technical preparations continued by the Committee; discussion
of the treaty by national legislatures and public
and private associations and entities; ratification
of the treaty by Argentina, Mexico, Paraguay,
and Peru; extension of Bolivia's time-limit for
adherence; examination by Colombia, Ecuador, and Venezuela of the possibility of their
accession to the association; application of the

treaty authorized by GATT at its seventeenth session. *October:* Inauguration of the Inter-American Development Bank. *December:* Signature of a general treaty of Central American Economic Integration by El Salvador, Guatemala, Honduras, and Nicaragua and agreement between these countries to establish a Central American Economic Integration Bank.

1961 *January-February:* Ratification of the Montevideo Treaty by Brazil and Chile. *March:* Announcement by the President of the United States of America of his country's intention of supporting Latin American economic integration, in relation with the general economic and social development of Latin America; further postponement of Bolivia's participation in the Montevideo Treaty. *May:* Instruments of ratification deposited by the signatory countries; in Chile, ninth session of ECLA and third session of the Trade Committee of ECLA; resolution requesting ECLA to study the relations between multilateral groups in Latin America and countries of the region still not members of those groups; decision of Ecuador to accede to the Latin American Free-Trade Association; submission of draft law to the Colombian Congress for the same purpose; deferment of decision by Venezuela; setting up in Honduras of the Central American Economic Integration Bank. *June:* Entry into force of the Montevideo Treaty on June 1; announcement of establishment of the Permanent Executive Committee, as well as of beginning of negotiations for the first annual reduction of tariff duties and other import restrictions.

APPENDIX B

TREATY ESTABLISHING A FREE-TRADE AREA AND INSTITUTING THE LATIN AMERICAN FREE-TRADE ASSOCIATION

(*Montevideo Treaty*)*

The Governments represented at the Inter-Governmental Conference for the Establishment of a Free-Trade Area among Latin American Countries,

Persuaded that the expansion of present national markets, through the gradual elimination of barriers to intra-regional trade, is a prerequisite if the Latin American countries are to accelerate their economic development process in such a way as to ensure a higher level of living for their peoples,

Aware that economic development should be attained through the maximum utilization of available production factors and the more effective coordination of the development programmes of the different production sectors in accordance

---

* As published in ECLA, *Economic Bulletin for Latin America,* Vol. V, No. 1, Santiago de Chile, March, 1960.

with norms which take due account of the interests of each and all and which makes proper compensation, by means of appropriate measures, for the special situation of countries which are at a relatively less advanced stage of economic development,

Convinced that the strengthening of national economies will contribute to the expansion of trade within Latin America and with the rest of the world,

Sure that, by the adoption of suitable formulas, conditions can be created that will be conducive to the gradual and smooth adaptation of existing productive activities to new patterns of reciprocal trade, and that further incentives will thereby be provided for the improvement and expansion of such trade,

Certain that any action to achieve such ends must take into account the commitments arising out of the international instruments which govern their trade,

Determined to persevere in their efforts to establish, gradually and progressively, a Latin American common market and, hence, to continue collaborating with the Latin American Governments as a whole in the work already initiated for this purpose, and

Motivated by the desire to pool their efforts to achieve the progressive complementarity and integration of their national economies on the basis of an effective reciprocity of benefits, decide to establish a Free-Trade Area and, to that end, to conclude a Treaty instituting the Latin American Free-Trade Association; and have, for this purpose, appointed their plenipotentiaries who have agreed as follows:

CHAPTER I

NAME AND PURPOSE

Article 1

By this Treaty the Contracting Parties establish a Free-Trade Area and institute the Latin American Free-Trade Association (hereinafter referred to as "the Association"), with headquarters in the city of Montevideo (Eastern Republic of Uruguay).

The term "Area", when used in this Treaty, means the combined territories of the Contracting Parties.

CHAPTER II

PROGRAMME FOR TRADE LIBERALIZATION

Article 2

The Free-Trade Area, established under the terms of the present Treaty, shall be brought into full operation within not more than twelve (12) years from the date of the Treaty's entry into force.

Article 3

During the period indicated in article 2, the Contracting Parties shall gradually eliminate, in respect of substantially all their reciprocal trade, such duties, charges and restrictions as may be applied to imports of goods originating in the territory of any Contracting Party.

For the purposes of the present Treaty the term "duties and charges" means customs duties and any other charges of equivalent effect—whether fiscal, monetary or exchange—that are levied on imports.

The provisions of the present article do not apply to fees and similar charges in respect of services rendered.

Article 4

The purpose set forth in article 3 shall be achieved through negotiations to be held from time to time among the Contracting Parties with a view to drawing up:

(*a*) National Schedules specifying the annual reductions in duties, charges and other restrictions which each Contracting Party grants to the other Contracting Parties in accordance with the provisions of article 5; and

(*b*) a Common Schedule listing the products on which the Contracting Parties collectively agree to eliminate duties, charges and other restrictions completely, so far as intra-Area trade is concerned, within the period mentioned in article 2, by complying with the minimum percentages set out in article 7 and through the gradual reduction provided for in article 5.

Article 5

With a view to the preparation of the National Schedules referred to in article 4, sub-paragraph (*a*), each Contracting Party shall annually grant to the other Contracting Parties reductions in duties and charges equivalent to not less than eight (8) per cent of the weighted average applicable to third countries, until they are eliminated in respect of substantially all of its imports from the Area, in accordance with the definitions, methods of calculation, rules and procedures laid down in the Protocol.

For this purpose, duties and charges for third parties shall be deemed to be those in force on 31 December prior to each negotiation.

When the import régime of a Contracting Party contains restrictions of such a kind that the requisite equivalence with the reductions in duties and charges granted by another Contracting Party or other Contracting Parties is unobtainable, the counterpart of these reductions shall be complemented by means of the elimination or relaxation of those restrictions.

Article 6

The National Schedules shall enter into force on 1 January of each year, except that those deriving from the initial negotiations shall enter into force on the date fixed by the Contracting Parties.

Article 7

The Common Schedule shall consist of products which, in terms of the aggregate value of the trade among the Contracting Parties, shall constitute not less than the following percentages, calculated in accordance with the provisions of the Protocol:

Twenty-five (25) per cent during the first three-year period;

Fifty (50) per cent during the second three-year period;

Seventy-five (75) per cent during the third three-year period;

Substantially all of such trade during the fourth three-year period.

Article 8

The inclusion of products in the Common Schedule shall be final and the concessions granted in respect thereof irrevocable.

Concessions granted in respect of products which appear only in the National Schedules may be withdrawn by negotiation among the Contracting Parties and on a basis of adequate compensation.

Article 9

The percentages referred to in articles 5 and 7 shall be calculated on the basis of the average annual value of trade during the three years preceding the year in which each negotiation is effected.

Article 10

The purpose of the negotiations—based on reciprocity of concessions—referred to in article 4 shall be to expand and diversify trade and to promote the progressive complementarity of the economies of the countries in the Area.

In these negotiations the situation of those Contracting Parties whose levels of duties, charges and restrictions differ substantially from those of the other Contracting Parties shall be considered with due fairness.

Article 11

If, as a result of the concessions granted, significant and persistent disadvantages are created in respect of trade between one Contracting Party and the others as a whole in the products included in the liberalization programme, the Contracting Parties shall, at the request of the Contracting Party affected, consider steps to remedy these disadvantages with a view to the adoption of suitable, non-restrictive measures designed to promote trade at the highest possible levels.

Article 12

If, as a result of circumstances other than those referred to in article 11, significant and persistent disadvantages are created in respect of trade in the products included in the liberalization programme, the Contracting Parties shall, at the request of the Contracting Party concerned, make every effort within their power to remedy these disadvantages.

Article 13

The reciprocity mentioned in article 10 refers to the expected growth in the flow of trade between each Contracting Party and the others as a whole, in the products included in the liberalization programme and those which may subsequently be added.

Chapter III

EXPANSION OF TRADE AND ECONOMIC COMPLEMENTARITY

Article 14

In order to ensure the continued expansion and diversification of reciprocal trade, the Contracting Parties shall take steps:

(*a*) to grant one another, while observing the principle of reciprocity, concessions which will ensure that, in the first negotiation, treatment not less favourable than that which existed before the date of entry into force of the present Treaty is accorded to imports from within the Area;

(*b*) to include in the National Schedules the largest possible number of products in which trade is carried on among the Contracting Parties; and

(*c*) to add to these Schedules an increasing number of products which are not yet included in reciprocal trade.

Article 15

In order to ensure fair competitive conditions among the Contracting Parties and to facilitate the increasing integration and complementarity of their economies, particularly with regard to industrial production, the Contracting Parties shall make every effort—in keeping with the liberalization objectives of the present Treaty—to reconcile their import and export régimes, as well as the treatment they accord to capital, goods and services from outside the Area.

Article 16

With a view to expediting the process of integration and complementarity referred to in article 15, the Contracting Parties:

(a) shall endeavour to promote progressively closer co-ordination of the corresponding industrialization policies, and shall sponsor for this purpose agreements among representatives of the economic sectors concerned; and

(b) may negotiate mutual agreements on complementarity by industrial sectors.

Article 17

The complementarity agreements referred to in article 16, subparagraph (b), shall set forth the liberalization programme to be applied to products of the sector concerned and may contain, *inter alia*, clauses designed to reconcile the treatment accorded to raw materials and other components used in the manufacture of these products.

Any Contracting Party concerned with the complementarity programmes shall be free to participate in the negotiation of these agreements.

The results of these negotiations shall, in every case, be embodied in protocols which shall enter into force after the Contracting Parties have decided that they are consistent with the general principles and purposes of the present Treaty.

CHAPTER IV

MOST-FAVOURED-NATION TREATMENT

Article 18

Any advantage, benefit, franchise, immunity or privilege applied by a Contracting Party in respect of a product originating in or intended for consignment to any other country shall be immediately and unconditionally extended to the similar product originating in or intended for consignment to the territory of the other Contracting Parties.

Article 19

The most-favoured-nation treatment referred to in article 18 shall not be applicable to the advantages, benefits, franchises, immunities and privileges already granted or which may be granted by virtue of agreements among Contracting Parties or between Contracting Parties and third countries with a view to facilitating border trade.

Article 20

Capital originating in the Area shall enjoy, in the territory of each Contracting Party, treatment not less favourable than that granted to capital originating in any other country.

CHAPTER V

TREATMENT IN RESPECT OF INTERNAL TAXATION

Article 21

With respect to taxes, rates and other internal duties and charges, products originating in the territory of a Contracting Party shall enjoy, in the territory of another Contracting Party, treatment no less favourable than that accorded to similar national products.

Article 22

Each Contracting Party shall endeavour to ensure that the charges or other domestic measures applied to products included in the liberalization programme which are not produced, or are produced only in small quantities, in its territory, do not nullify or reduce any concession or advantage obtained by any Contracting Party during the negotiations.

If a Contracting Party considers itself injured by virtue of the measures mentioned in the previous paragraph, it may appeal to the competent organs of the Association with a view to having the matter examined and appropriate recommendations made.

CHAPTER VI

SAVING CLAUSES

Article 23

The Contracting Parties may, as a provisional measure and providing that the customary level of consumption in the importer country is not thereby lowered, authorize a Contracting Party to impose non-discriminatory restrictions upon imports of products included in the liberalization programme which originate in the Area, if these products are imported in such quantities or under such conditions that they have, or are liable to have, serious repercussions on specific productive activities of vital importance to the national economy.

Article 24

The Contracting Parties may likewise authorize a Contracting Party which has adopted measures to correct its unfavourable over-all balance of payments to extend these measures, provisionally and without discrimination, to intra-Area trade in the products included in the liberalization programme.

The Contracting Parties shall endeavour to ensure that the imposition of restrictions deriving from the balance-of-payments situation does not affect trade, within the Area, in the products included in the liberalization programme.

Article 25

If the situations referred to in articles 23 and 24 call for immediate action, the Contracting Party concerned may, as an emergency arrangement to be referred to the Contracting Parties, apply the measures provided for in the said articles. The measures adopted must immediately be communicated to the Committee mentioned in article 33, which, if it deems necessary, shall convene a special session of the Conference.

Article 26

Should the measures envisaged in this chapter be prolonged for more than one year, the Committee shall propose to the

Conference, referred to in article 33, either *ex officio* or at the request of any of the Contracting Parties, the immediate initiation of negotiations with a view to eliminating the restrictions adopted.

The present article does not affect the provisions of article 8.

Chapter VII

SPECIAL PROVISIONS CONCERNING AGRICULTURE

Article 27

The Contracting Parties shall seek to co-ordinate their agricultural development and agricultural commodity trade policies, with a view to securing the most efficient utilization of their natural resources, raising the standard of living of the rural population, and guaranteeing normal supplies to consumers, without disorganizing the regular productive activities of each Contracting Party.

Article 28

Providing that no lowering of its customary consumption or increase in anti-economic production is involved, a Contracting Party may apply, within the period mentioned in article 2, and in respect of trade in agricultural commodities of substantial importance to its economy that are included in the liberalization programme, appropriate non-discriminatory measures designed to

(a) limit imports to the amount required to meet the deficit in internal production; and

(b) equalize the prices of the imported and domestic product.

The Contracting Party which decides to apply these measures shall inform the other Contracting Parties before it puts them into effect.

Article 29

During the period prescribed in article 2 an attempt shall be made to expand intra-Area trade in agricultural commodities by such means as agreements among the Contracting Parties designed to cover deficits in domestic production.

For this purpose, the Contracting Parties shall give priority, under normal competitive conditions, to products originating in the territories of the other Contracting Parties, due consideration being given to the traditional flows of intra-Area trade.

Should such agreements be concluded among two or more Contracting Parties, the other Contracting Parties shall be notified before the agreements enter into force.

Article 30

The measures provided for in this chapter shall not be applied for the purpose of incorporating, in the production of agricultural commodities, resources which imply a reduction in the average level of productivity existing on the date on which the present Treaty enters into force.

Article 31

If a Contracting Party considers itself injured by a reduction of its exports attributable to the lowering of the usual consumption level of the importer country as a result of the measures referred to in article 28 and/or an anti-economic increase in the production referred to in the previous article, it may appeal to the competent organs of the Association to study the situation and, if necessary, to make recommendations for the adoption of appropriate measures to be applied in accordance with article 12.

CHAPTER VIII

MEASURES IN FAVOUR OF COUNTRIES AT A
RELATIVELY LESS ADVANCED STAGE OF
ECONOMIC DEVELOPMENT

Article 32

The Contracting Parties, recognizing that fulfilment of the purpose of the present Treaty will be facilitated by the economic growth of the countries in the Area that are at a relatively less advanced stage of economic development, shall take steps to create conditions conducive to such growth.

To this end, the Contracting Parties may:

(*a*) authorize a Contracting Party to grant to another Contracting Party which is at a relatively less advanced stage of economic development within the Area, as long as necessary and as a temporary measure, for the purposes set out in the present article, advantages not extended to the other Contracting Parties, in order to encourage the introduction or expansion of specific productive activities;

(*b*) authorize a Contracting Party at a relatively less advanced stage of economic development within the Area to implement the programme for the reduction of duties, charges and other restrictions under more favourable conditions, specially agreed upon;

(*c*) authorize a Contracting Party at a relatively less advanced stage of economic development within the Area to adopt appropriate measures to correct an unfavourable balance of payments, if the case arises;

(d) authorize a Contracting Party at a relatively less advanced stage of economic development within the Area to apply, if necessary and as a temporary measure, and providing that this does not entail a decrease in its customary consumption, appropriate non-discriminatory measures designed to protect the domestic output of products included in the liberalization programme which are of vital importance to its economic development;

(e) make collective arrangements in favour of a Contracting Party at a relatively less advanced stage of economic development within the Area with respect to the support and promotion, both inside and outside the Area, of financial or technical measures designed to bring about the expansion of existing productive activities or to encourage new activities, particularly those intended for the industrialization of its raw materials; and

(f) promote or support, as the case may be, special technical assistance programmes for one or more Contracting Parties, intended to raise, in countries at a relatively less advanced stage of economic development within the Area, productivity levels in specific production sectors.

Chapter IX

ORGANS OF THE ASSOCIATION

Article 33

The organs of the Association are the Conference of the Contracting Parties (referred to in this Treaty as "the Conference") and the Standing Executive Committee (referred to in this Treaty as "the Committee").

Article 34

The Conference is the supreme organ of the Association. It shall adopt all decisions in matters requiring joint action on the part of the Contracting Parties, and it shall be empowered, *inter alia:*

(*a*) to take the necessary steps to carry out the present Treaty and to study the results of its implementation;

(*b*) to promote the negotiations provided for in article 4 and to assess the results thereof;

(*c*) to approve the Committee's annual budget and to fix the contributions of each Contracting Party;

(*d*) to lay down its own rules of procedure and to approve the Committee's rules of procedure;

(*e*) to elect a Chairman and two Vice-Chairmen for each session;

(*f*) to appoint the Executive Secretary of the Committee; and

(*g*) to deal with other business of common interest.

Article 35

The Conference shall be composed of duly accredited representatives of the Contracting Parties. Each delegation shall have one vote.

Article 36

The Conference shall hold: (*a*) a regular session once a year; and (*b*) special sessions when convened by the Committee.

At each session the Conference shall decide the place and date of the following regular session.

Article 37

The Conference may not take decisions unless at least two-thirds (2/3) of the Contracting Parties are present.

Article 38

During the first two years in which the present Treaty is in force, decisions of the Conference shall be adopted when affirmative votes are cast by at least two-thirds (2/3) of the Contracting Parties and providing that no negative vote is cast.

The Contracting Parties shall likewise determine the voting system to be adopted after this two-year period.

The affirmative vote of two-thirds (2/3) of the Contracting Parties shall be required:

(*a*) to approve the Committee's annual budget;
(*b*) to elect the Chairman and Vice-Chairmen of the Conference, as well as the Executive Secretary; and
(*c*) to fix the time and place of the sessions of the Conference.

Article 39

The Committee is the permanent organ of the Association responsible for supervising the implementation of the provisions of the present Treaty. Its duties and responsibilities shall be, *inter alia*:

(*a*) to convene the Conference;
(*b*) to submit for the approval of the Conference an annual work programme and the Committee's annual budget estimates;
(*c*) to represent the Association in dealings with third

countries and international organs and entities for the purpose of considering matters of common interest. It shall also represent the Association in contracts and other instruments of public and private law;

(d) to undertake studies, to suggest measures and to submit to the Conference such recommendations as it deems appropriate for the effective implementation of the Treaty;

(e) to submit to the Conference at its regular sessions an annual report on its activities and on the results of the implementation of the present Treaty;

(f) to request the technical advice and the co-operation of individuals and of national and international organizations;

(g) to take such decisions as may be delegated to it by the Conference; and

(h) to undertake the work assigned to it by the Conference.

Article 40

The Committee shall consist of a Permanent Representative of each Contracting Party, who shall have a single vote.

Each Representative shall have an Alternate.

Article 41

The Committee shall have a Secretariat headed by an Executive Secretary and comprising technical and administrative personnel.

The Executive Secretary, elected by the Conference for a three-year term and re-eligible for similar periods, shall attend the plenary meetings of the Committee without the right to vote.

The Executive Secretary shall be the General Secretary of the Conference. His duties shall be, *inter alia:*

(*a*) to organize the work of the Conference and of the Committee;

(*b*) to prepare the Committee's annual budget estimates; and

(*c*) to recruit and engage the technical and administrative staff in accordance with the Committee's rules of procedure.

Article 42

In the performance of their duties, the Executive Secretary and the Secretariat staff shall not seek or receive instructions from any Government or from any other national or international entity. They shall refrain from any action which might reflect on their position as international civil servants.

The Contracting Parties undertake to respect the international character of the responsibilities of the Executive Secretary and of the Secretariat staff and shall refrain from influencing them in any way in the discharge of their responsibilities.

Article 43

In order to facilitate the study of specific problems, the Committee may set up Advisory Commissions composed of representatives of the various sectors of economic activity of each of the Contracting Parties.

Article 44

The Committee shall request, for the organs of the Association, the technical advice of the secretariat of the United Nations

Economic Commission for Latin America (ECLA) and of the Inter-American Economic and Social Council (IA-ECOSOC) of the Organization of American States.

Article 45

The Committee shall be constituted sixty days from the entry into force of the present Treaty and shall have its headquarters in the city of Montevideo.

Chapter X

JURIDICAL PERSONALITY—IMMUNITIES AND PRIVILEGES

Article 46

The Latin American Free-Trade Association shall possess complete juridical personality and shall, in particular, have the power:

(*a*) to contract;
(*b*) to acquire and dispose of the movable and immovable property it needs for the achievement of its objectives;
(*c*) to institute legal proceedings; and
(*d*) to hold funds in any currency and to transfer them as necessary.

Article 47

The representatives of the Contracting Parties and the international staff and advisers of the Association shall enjoy in the Area such diplomatic and other immunities and privileges as are necessary for the exercise of their functions.

The Contracting Parties undertake to conclude, as soon as possible, an Agreement regulating the provisions of the previous paragraph in which the aforesaid privileges and immunities shall be defined.

The Association shall conclude with the Government of the Eastern Republic of Uruguay an Agreement for the purpose of specifying the privileges and immunities which the Association, its organs and its international staff and advisers shall enjoy.

Chapter XI

MISCELLANEOUS PROVISIONS

Article 48

No change introduced by a Contracting Party in its régime of import duties and charges shall imply a level of duties and charges less favourable than that in force before the change for any commodity in respect of which concessions are granted to the other Contracting Parties.

The requirement set out in the previous paragraph shall not apply to the conversion to present worth of the official base value (*aforo*) in respect of customs duties and charges, providing that such conversion corresponds exclusively to the real value of the goods. In such cases, the value shall not include the customs duties and charges levied on the goods.

Article 49

In order to facilitate the implementation of the provisions of the present Treaty, the Contracting Parties shall, as soon as possible:

   (*a*) determine the criteria to be adopted for the purpose of establishing the origin of goods and for classifying them as raw materials, semimanufactured goods or finished products;

(*b*) simplify and standardize procedures and formalities relating to reciprocal trade;

(*c*) prepare a tariff nomenclature to serve as a common basis for the presentation of statistics and for carrying out the negotiations provided for in the present Treaty;

(*d*) determine what shall be deemed to constitute border trade within the meaning of article 19;

(*e*) determine the criteria for the purpose of defining "dumping" and other unfair trade practices and the procedures relating thereto.

Article 50

The products imported from the Area by a Contracting Party may not be re-exported save by agreement between the Contracting Parties concerned.

A product shall not be deemed to be a re-export if it has been subjected in the importer country to industrial processing or manufacture, the degree of which shall be determined by the Committee.

Article 51

Products imported or exported by a Contracting Party shall enjoy freedom of transit within the Area and shall only be subject to the payment of the normal rates for services rendered.

Article 52

No Contracting Party shall promote its exports by means of subsidies or other measures likely to disrupt normal competitive conditions in the Area.

An export shall not be deemed to have been subsidized if it is exempted from duties and charges levied on the product or its components when destined for internal consumption, or if it is subject to drawback.

Article 53

No provision of the present Treaty shall be so construed as to constitute an impediment to the adoption and execution of measures relating to:

(*a*) the protection of public morality;

(*b*) the application of security laws and regulations;

(*c*) the control of imports or exports of arms, ammunition and other war equipment and, in exceptional circumstances, of all other military items, in so far as this is compatible with the terms of article 51 and of the treaties on the unrestricted freedom of transit in force among the Contracting Parties;

(*d*) the protection of human, animal and plant life and health;

(*e*) imports and exports of gold and silver bullion;

(*f*) the protection of the nation's heritage of artistic, historical and archaeological value; and

(*g*) the export, use and consumption of nuclear materials, radio-active products or any other material that may be used in the development of exploitation of nuclear energy.

Article 54

The Contracting Parties shall make every effort to direct their policies with a view to creating conditions favourable to the establishment of a Latin American common market. To that end, the Committee shall undertake studies and consider projects and plans designed to achieve this purpose, and shall endeavour to co-ordinate its work with that of other international organizations.

CHAPTER XII

FINAL PROVISIONS

Article 55

The present Treaty may not be signed with reservations nor shall reservations be admitted at the time of ratification or accession.

Article 56

The present Treaty shall be ratified by the signatory States at the earliest opportunity.

The instruments of ratification shall be deposited with the Government of the Eastern Republic of Uruguay, which shall communicate the date of deposit to the Governments of the signatory and successively acceding States.

Article 57

The present Treaty shall enter into force for the first three ratifying States thirty days after the third instrument of ratification has been deposited; and, for the other signatories, thirty days after the respective instrument of ratification has been deposited, and in the order in which the ratifications are deposited.

The Government of the Eastern Republic of Uruguay shall communicate the date of the entry into force of the present Treaty to the Government of each of the signatory States.

Article 58

Following its entry into force, the present Treaty shall remain open to accession by the other Latin American States, which for this purpose shall deposit the relevant instrument of accession with the Government of the Eastern Republic of Uruguay. The Treaty shall enter into force for the acceding State thirty days after the deposit of the corresponding instrument.

Acceding States shall enter into the negotiations referred to in article 4 at the session of the Conference immediately following the date of deposit of the instrument of accession.

Article 59

Each Contracting Party shall begin to benefit from the concessions already granted to one another by the other Contracting Parties as from the date of entry into force of the reductions in duties and charges and other restrictions negotiated by them on a basis of reciprocity, and after the minimum obligations referred to in article 5, accumulated during the period which has elapsed since the entry into force of the present Treaty, have been carried out.

Article 60

The Contracting Parties may present amendments to the present Treaty, which shall be set out in protocols that shall enter into force upon their ratification by all the Contracting Parties and after the corresponding instruments have been deposited.

Article 61

On the expiry of the twelve-year term starting on the date of entry into force of the present Treaty, the Contracting Parties shall proceed to study the results of the Treaty's implementation and shall initiate the necessary collective negotiations with a view to fulfilling more effectively the purposes of the Treaty and, if desirable, to adapting it to a new stage of economic integration.

Article 62

The provisions of the present Treaty shall not affect the rights and obligations deriving from agreements signed by any of the Contracting Parties prior to the entry into force of the present Treaty.

However, each Contracting Party shall take the necessary steps to reconcile the provisions of existing agreements with the purposes of the present Treaty.

Article 63

The present Treaty shall be of unlimited duration.

Article 64

A Contracting Party wishing to withdraw from the present Treaty shall inform the other Contracting Parties of its intention at a regular session of the Conference, and shall formally submit the instrument of denunciation at the following regular session.

When the formalities of denunciation have been completed, those rights and obligations of the denouncing Government which derive from its status as a Contracting Party shall cease automatically, with the exception of those relating to reductions in duties and charges and other restrictions, received or granted under the liberalization programme, which shall remain in force for a period of five years from the date on which the denunciation becomes formally effective.

The period specified in the preceding paragraph may be shortened if there is sufficient justification, with the consent of the Conference and at the request of the Contracting Party concerned.

Article 65

The present Treaty shall be called the Montevideo Treaty.

In witness whereof the undersigned Plenipotentiaries, having deposited their full powers, found in good and due form, have signed the present Treaty on behalf of their respective Governments.

Done in the city of Montevideo, on the eighteenth day of the month of February in the year one thousand nine hundred and sixty, in one original in the Spanish and one in the Portuguese language, both texts being equally authentic. The Government of the Eastern Republic of Uruguay shall be the depositary of the present Treaty and shall transmit duly certified copies thereof to the Governments of the other signatory and acceding States.

For the Government of the Argentine Republic:

(*Signed*) *Diógenes Taboada*

For the Government of the United States
of Brazil:

(*Signed*) *Horacio Lafer*

For the Government of the Republic of Chile:

(*Signed*) *Germán Vergara Donoso*

For the Government of the Republic of the
United Mexican States:

(*Signed*) *Manuel Tello*

For the Government of the Republic of Paraguay:

(*Signed*) *Raúl Sapena Pastor*
Pedro Ramón Chamorro

For the Government of Peru:

(*Signed*) *Hernán Bellido*
Gonzalo L. de Aramburu

For the Government of the Eastern Republic
of Uruguay:

(*Signed*) *Horacio Martínez Montero*
Mateo Magariños de Mello

Protocol No. 1

ON NORMS AND PROCEDURES
FOR NEGOTIATIONS

On the occasion of the signing of the Treaty establishing a
free-trade area and instituting the Latin American Free-Trade
Association (Montevideo Treaty), the signatories, thereunto
duly authorized by their Governments, hereby agree upon the
following Protocol:

TITLE I

Calculation of weighted averages

1. For the purposes of article 5 of the Montevideo Treaty, it
shall be understood that, as a result of the negotiations for the
establishment of the National Schedules, the difference between the weighted average of duties and charges in force for

third countries and that which shall be applicable to imports from within the area shall be not less than the product of eight per cent (8%) of the weighted average of duties and charges in force for third countries multiplied by the number of years that have elapsed since the Treaty became effective.

2. The reduction mechanism shall therefore be based on two weighted averages: one corresponding to the average of the duties and charges in force for third countries; and the other to the average of the duties and charges which shall be applicable to imports from within the Area.

3. In order to calculate each of these weighted averages, the total amount that would be represented by the duties and charges on aggregate imports of the goods under consideration shall be divided by the total value of these imports.

4. This calculation will give a percentage (or *ad valorem* figure) for each weighted average. It is the difference between the two averages that shall be not less than the product of the factor 0.08 (or eight per cent) multiplied by the number of years elapsed.

5. The foregoing formula is expressed as follows:

$$t \leqslant T \ (1-0.08n) \text{ in which}$$

$t =$ weighted average of the duties and charges that shall be applicable to imports from within the area;

$T =$ weighted average of duties and charges in force for third countries;

$n =$ number of years since the Treaty entered into force.

6. In calculating the weighted averages for each of the Contracting Parties, the following shall be taken into account:

(*a*) Products originating in the territory of the other Contracting Parties and imported from the Area during the preceding three-year period and further products included in the National Schedule concerned as a result of negotiations;

(*b*) The total value of imports, irrespective of origin, of each of the products referred to in sub-paragraph (*a*), during the three-year period preceding each negotiation; and

(*c*) The duties and charges on imports from third countries in force as on 31 December prior to the negotiations, and the duties and charges applicable to imports from within the Area entering into force on 1 January following the negotiations.

7. The Contracting Parties shall be entitled to exclude products of little value from the group referred to in sub-paragraph (*a*), provided that their aggregate value does not exceed five per cent (5%) of the value of imports from within the Area.

TITLE II

Exchange of information

8. The Contracting Parties shall provide one another, through the Standing Executive Committee, with information as complete as possible on:

(*a*) National statistics in respect of total imports and exports (value in dollars and volume, by countries both of origin and of destination), production and consumption;

(*b*) Customs legislation and regulations;

(*c*) Exchange, monetary, fiscal and administrative legislation, regulations and practices bearing on exports and imports;

(*d*) International trade treaties and agreements whose provisions relate to the Treaty;

(*e*) Systems of direct or indirect subsidies on production or exports, including minimum price systems; and

(*f*) State trading systems.

9. So far as possible, these data shall be permanently available to the Contracting Parties. They shall be specially brought up to date sufficiently in advance of the opening of the annual negotiations.

TITLE III

Negotiation of National Schedules

10. Before 30 June of each year, the Contracting Parties shall make available to one another, through the Standing Executive Committee, the list of products in respect of which they are applying for concessions and, before 15 August of each year (with the exception of the first year, when the corresponding final date shall be 1 October), the preliminary list of items in favour of which they are prepared to grant concessions.

11. On 1 September of each year (with the exception of the first year, when the corresponding date shall be 1 November), the Contracting Parties shall initiate the negotiation of the concessions to be accorded by each to the others as a whole. The concessions shall be assessed multilaterally, although this shall not preclude the conduct of negotiations by pairs or groups of countries, in accordance with the interest attaching to specific products.

12. Upon the conclusion of this phase of the negotiations, the Standing Executive Committee shall make the calculations referred to in title I of this Protocol and shall inform each Contracting Party, at the earliest possible opportunity, of the percentage whereby its individual concessions reduce the weighted average of the duties and charges in force for imports from within the Area, in relation to the weighted average of duties and charges applicable in the case of third countries.

13. When the concessions negotiated fall short of the corresponding minimum commitment, the negotiations among the Contracting Parties shall be continued, so that the list of reductions of duties and charges and other restrictions to enter into force as from the following 1 January may be simultaneously published by each of the Contracting Parties not later than 1 November of each year.

Title IV

Negotiation of the Common Schedule

14. During each three-year period and not later than on 31 May of the third, sixth, ninth and twelfth years from the time of the Treaty's entry into force, the Standing Executive Committee shall supply the Contracting Parties with statistical data on the value and volume of the products traded in the Area during the preceding three-year period, indicating the proportion of aggregate trade which each individually represented.

15. Before 30 June of the third, sixth and ninth years from the time of the Treaty's entry into force, the Contracting Parties shall exchange the lists of products whose inclusion in the Common Schedule they wish to negotiate.

16. The Contracting Parties shall conduct multilateral negotiations to establish, before 30 November in the third, sixth, ninth and twelfth years, a Common Schedule comprising goods whose value meets the minimum commitments referred to in article 7 of the Treaty.

Title V

Special and temporary provisions

17. In the negotiations to which this Protocol refers, consideration shall be given to those cases in which varying levels of duties and charges on certain products create conditions such that producers in the Area are not competing on equitable terms.

18. To this end, steps shall be taken to ensure prior equalization of tariffs or to secure by any other suitable procedure the highest possible degree of effective reciprocity.

In witness whereof the respective representatives have signed the Protocol.

Done at the City of Montevideo, on the eighteenth day of

the month of February in the year one thousand nine hundred and sixty, in one original in the Spanish and one in the Portuguese language, both texts being equally authentic.

The Government of the Eastern Republic of Uruguay shall act as depositary of the present Protocol and shall send certified true copies thereof to the Governments of the other signatory and acceding countries.

For the Government of the Argentine Republic:

Diógenes Taboada

For the Government of the Republic of the United States of Brazil:

Horacio Lafer

For the Government of the Republic of Chile:

Germán Vergara Donoso

For the Government of the Republic of the United Mexican States:

Manuel Tello

For the Government of the Republic of Paraguay:

Raúl Sapena Pastor
Pedro Ramón Chamorro

For the Government of Peru:

Hernán Bellido
Gonzalo L. de Aramburu

For the Government of the Eastern Republic of Uruguay:

Horacio Martínez Montero
Mateo Magariños de Mello

Protocol No. 2

ON THE ESTABLISHMENT
OF A PROVISIONAL COMMITTEE

On the occasion of the signing of the Treaty establishing a free-trade area and instituting the Latin American Free-Trade Association (Montevideo Treaty), the signatories, thereunto duly authorized by their Governments, taking into consideration the need to adopt and coordinate measures to facilitate the entry into force of the Treaty, hereby agree as follows:

1. A Provisional Committee shall be set up, composed of one representative of each signatory State. Each representative shall have an alternate.

At its first meeting the Provisional Committee shall elect from among its members one Chairman and two Vice-Chairmen.

2. The terms of reference of the Provisional Committee shall be as follows:

   (*a*) To draw up its rules of procedure;
   (*b*) To prepare, within sixty days from the date of its inauguration, its work programme, and to establish its budget of expenditure and the contributions to be made by each country;
   (*c*) To adopt the measures and prepare the documents necessary for the presentation of the Treaty to the Contracting Parties of the General Agreement on Tariffs and Trade (GATT);
   (*d*) To convene and prepare for the first Conference of Contracting Parties;
   (*e*) To assemble and prepare the data and statistics required for the first series of negotiations connected with the implementation of the liberalization programme provided for in the Treaty;

(*f*) To carry out or promote studies and research, and to adopt whatsoever measures may be necessary in the common interest during its period of office; and

(*g*) To prepare a preliminary draft agreement on the privileges and immunities referred to in article 47 of the Treaty.

3. In technical matters, the Provisional Committee shall be assisted in an advisory capacity by the United Nations Economic Commission for Latin America (ECLA) and the Inter-American Economic and Social Council (IA-ECOSOC), of the Organization of American States, in accordance with the relevant Protocol.

4. The Provisional Committee shall appoint an Administrative Secretary and other requisite staff.

5. The Provisional Committee shall be inaugurated on 1 April 1960, and its quorum shall be constituted by not less than four members. Up to that date, the Officers of the Inter-Governmental Conference for the Establishment of a Free-Trade Area among Latin American Countries shall continue to discharge their functions, for the sole purpose of establishing the Provisional Committee.

6. The Provisional Committee shall remain in office until the Standing Executive Committee, provided for in article 33 of the Treaty, has been set up.

7. The Provisional Committee shall have its headquarters in the City of Montevideo.

8. The Officers of the above-mentioned Conference are recommended to request the Government of the Eastern Republic of Uruguay to advance the necessary sums to cover the payment of staff salaries and the installation and operational expenses of the Provisional Committee during the first ninety days. These sums shall be subsequently reimbursed by the States signatories of the present Treaty.

9. The Provisional Committee shall approach the signatory

Governments with a view to obtaining for the members of its constituent delegations, as well as for its international staff and advisers, such immunities and privileges as may be needful for the performance of their duties.

In witness whereof the respective representatives have signed the present Protocol.

Done at the City of Montevideo, on the eighteenth day of the month of February in the year one thousand nine hundred and sixty, in one original in the Spanish and one in the Portuguese language, both texts being equally authentic. The Government of the Eastern Republic of Uruguay shall act as the depositary of the present Protocol and shall send certified true copies thereof to the Governments of the other signatory and acceding countries.

For the Government of the Argentine Republic:

Diógenes Taboada

For the Government of the Republic of the United States of Brazil:

Horacio Lafer

For the Government of the Republic of Chile:

Germán Vergara Donoso

For the Government of the Republic of the United Mexican States:

Manuel Tello

For the Government of the Republic of Paraguay:

Raúl Sapena Pastor
Pedro Ramón Chamorro

For the Government of Peru:

Hernán Bellido
Gonzalo L. de Aramburu

For the Government of the Eastern
Republic of Uruguay:

Horacio Martínez Montero
Mateo Magariños de Mello

Protocol No. 3

ON THE COLLABORATION OF THE UNITED NATIONS ECONOMIC COMMISSION FOR LATIN AMERICA (ecla) AND OF THE INTER-AMERICAN ECONOMIC AND SOCIAL COUNCIL (ia-ecosoc) OF THE ORGANIZATION OF AMERICAN STATES

On the occasion of the signing of the Treaty establishing a free-trade area and instituting the Latin American Free-Trade Association (Montevideo Treaty), the signatories, thereunto duly authorized by their Governments, hereby agree as follows:

1. With reference to the provisions of article 44 of the Treaty and in view of the fact that the secretariats of ecla and of ia-ecosoc have agreed to assist the organs of the Latin American Free-Trade Association with advice on technical matters, a representative of each of the secretariats in question shall attend the meetings of the Standing Executive Committee of the above-mentioned Association when the business to be discussed is, in the Committee's opinion, of a technical nature.

2. The appointment of the representatives referred to shall be subject to the prior approval of the members of the said Committee.

In witness whereof the respective representatives have signed the present Protocol.

Done at the City of Montevideo, on the eighteenth day of the month of February in the year one thousand nine hundred and sixty, in one original in the Spanish and one in the Portuguese language, both texts being equally authentic. The Government of the Eastern Republic of Uruguay shall act as the depositary of the present Protocol and shall send certified true copies thereof to the Governments of the other signatory and acceding countries.

For the Government of the Argentine Republic:

Diógenes Taboada

For the Government of the Republic of the
United States of Brazil:

Horacio Lafer

For the Government of the Republic of Chile:

Germán Vergara Donoso

For the Government of the Republic of the
United Mexican States:

Manuel Tello

For the Government of the Republic of Paraguay:

Raúl Sapena Pastor
Pedro Ramón Chamorro

For the Government of Peru:

Hernán Bellido
Gonzalo L. de Aramburu

For the Government of the Eastern
Republic of Uruguay:

Horacio Martínez Montero
Mateo Magariños de Mello

Protocol No. 4

ON COMMITMENTS TO PURCHASE OR SELL PETROLEUM AND PETROLEUM DERIVATIVES

On the occasion of the signing of the Treaty establishing a free-trade area and instituting the Latin American Free-Trade Association (Montevideo Treaty), the signatories, thereunto duly authorized by their Governments, hereby agree:

To declare that the provisions of the Montevideo Treaty, signed on 18 February 1960, are not applicable to commitments to purchase or sell petroleum and petroleum derivatives resulting from agreements concluded by the signatories of the present Protocol prior to the date of signature of the above-mentioned Treaty.

In witness whereof the respective representatives have signed the present Protocol.

Done at the City of Montevideo, on the eighteenth day of the month of February in the year one thousand nine hundred and sixty, in one original in the Spanish and one in the Portuguese language, both texts being equally authentic.

The Government of the Eastern Republic of Uruguay shall act as depositary of the present Protocol and shall send certified true copies thereof to the Governments of the other signatory and acceding countries.

For the Government of the Argentine Republic:

Diógenes Taboada

For the Government of the Republic of the United States of Brazil:

Horacio Lafer

For the Government of the Republic of Chile:

Germán Vergara Donoso

For the Government of the Republic of the
United Mexican States:

Manuel Tello

For the Government of the Republic of Paraguay:

Raúl Sapena Pastor
Pedro Ramón Chamorro

For the Government of Peru:

Hernán Bellido
Gonzalo L. de Aramburu

For the Government of the Eastern
Republic of Uruguay:

Horacio Martínez Montero
Mateo Magariños de Mello

Protocol No. 5

ON SPECIAL TREATMENT IN FAVOUR
OF BOLIVIA AND PARAGUAY

On the occasion of the signing of the Treaty establishing a
free-trade area and instituting the Latin American Free-Trade
Association (Montevideo Treaty), the signatories, thereunto
duly authorized by their Governments hereby agree:

To declare that Bolivia and Paraguay are at present in a
position to invoke in their favour the provisions in the Treaty
concerning special treatment for countries at a relatively less
advanced stage of economic development within the Free-Trade
Area.

In witness whereof the respective representatives have
signed the present Protocol.

Done at the City of Montevideo, on the eighteenth day of
the month of February in the year one thousand nine hundred

and sixty, in one original in the Spanish and one in the Portuguese language, both texts being equally authentic.

The Government of the Eastern Republic of Uruguay shall act as depositary of the present Protocol and shall send certified true copies thereof to the Governments of the other signatory and acceding countries.

For the Government of the Argentine Republic:
Diógenes Taboada

For the Government of the Republic of the
United States of Brazil:

Horacio Lafer

For the Government of the Republic of Chile:
Germán Vergara Donoso

For the Government of the Republic of the
United Mexican States:

Manuel Tello

For the Government of the Republic of Paraguay:
Raúl Sopena Pastor
Pedro Ramón Chamorro

For the Government of Peru:
Hernán Bellido
Gonzalo L. de Aramburu

For the Government of the Eastern
Republic of Uruguay:

Horacio Martínez Montero
Mateo Magariños de Mello

Resolution I

MEETINGS OF GOVERNMENTAL
REPRESENTATIVES OF CENTRAL BANKS

*The Inter-Governmental Conference for the Establishment of
a Free-Trade Area among Latin American Countries,*

In view of the report submitted to the Conference by the
Meeting of Governmental Representatives of Central Banks,
held at Montevideo in January 1960,

Considering the desirability of continuing the studies on
payments and credits to facilitate the financing of intra-Area
transactions and therefore the fulfilment of the purposes of the
Treaty establishing a Free-Trade Area and instituting the Latin
American Free-Trade Association.

Decides:

1. To take note of the above-mentioned report;

2. To request the Provisional Committee to convene informal
meetings of governmental experts from the central banks of
Argentina, Bolivia, Brazil, Chile, Mexico, Paraguay, Peru and
Uruguay, which shall be organized by the secretariat of the
United Nations Economic Commission for Latin America
(ECLA);

3. To establish that the object of these meetings shall be the
continuance of the studies on credits and payments to facilitate
the financing of intra-Area transactions and therefore the fulfilment of the purposes of the aforesaid Treaty;

4. To request the United Nations Economic Commission for
Latin America (ECLA), the Inter-American Economic and Central Council (IA-ECOSOC) of the Organization of American

States and the International Monetary Fund for their advice and technical assistance;

5. To extend the invitation to experts from the central banks of such countries as may have acceded to the said Treaty.

Montevideo, 18 February 1960.

For the Government of the Argentine Republic:

Diógenes Taboada

For the Government of the Republic of the United States of Brazil:

Horacio Lafer

For the Government of the Republic of Chile:

Germán Vergara Donoso

For the Government of the Republic of the United Mexican States:

Manuel Tello

For the Government of the Republic of Paraguay:

Raúl Sapena Pastor
Pedro Ramón Chamorro

For the Government of Peru:

Hernán Bellido
Gonzalo L. de Aramburu

For the Government of the Eastern Republic of Uruguay:

Horacio Martínez Montero
Mateo Magariños de Mello

Resolution II

MORATORIUM GRANTED TO BOLIVIA FOR SIGNATURE OF THE TREATY

The Inter-Governmental Conference for the Establishment of a Free-Trade Area among Latin American Countries,

Considering the generous spirit of co-operation displayed by Bolivia in its participation in the negotiations for the conclusion of the Treaty establishing a Free-Trade Area and instituting the Latin American Free-Trade Association,

Mindful of the motives adduced by the delegation of Bolivia to explain why, for reasons of *force majeure,* it is unable to sign the above-mentioned Treaty on the present occasion,

Decides to grant the Government of Bolivia a moratorium of four (4) months during which it will be free to accede to the aforesaid Treaty as a signatory State.

Montevideo, 18 February 1960.

For the Government of the Argentine Republic:

Diógenes Taboada

For the Government of the Republic of the United States of Brazil:

Horacio Lafer

For the Government of the Republic of Chile:

Germán Vergara Donoso

For the Government of the Republic of the United Mexican States:

Manuel Tello

For the Government of the Republic of Paraguay:

Raúl Sapena Pastor
Pedro Ramón Chamorro

For the Government of Peru:

Hernán Bellido
Gonzalo L. de Aramburu

For the Government of the Eastern
Republic of Uruguay:

Horacio Martínez Montero
Mateo Magariños de Mello

SELECTED BIBLIOGRAPHY

SELECTED BIBLIOGRAPHY

COMMON MARKET, FREE TRADE AREA, AND GENERAL ASPECTS

Campos Salas, Octaviano. "Comercio interlatinoamericano e integración regional," * *Comercio Exterior.* México, Banco Nacional de Comercio Exterior, October 1959.
————, "La zona de libre comercio en América Latina," *Comercio Exterior.* México, March 1960.
Cárdenas, José C. "El mercado común latinoamericano y sus proyecciones en el desarrollo regional y nacional," *Boletín Trimestral de Informaciones Económicas.* Quito, Editorial Universitaria, March 1959, pp. 32–73.
Committee for Economic Development. *Cooperation for Progress in Latin America.* New York, April 1961.
Dell, Sidney S. "El tratado de Montevideo," *Suplemento al*

---

* Titles cited in Spanish or Portuguese are not available in English translation.

Boletín Quincenal. México, Centro de Estudios Monetarios Latinoamericanos, April 1960, pp. 89–92.

——, *Problemas de un mercado común latinoamericano.* México, Centro de Estudios Monetarios Latinoamericanos, 1959.

Dosik, Richard S. "The Montevideo Treaty and 'New' Trade," *Inter-American Economic Affairs,* Vol. 14, No. 3. Washington, D.C., 1960.

Echeverría, Vicente. "La integración económica regional en América Latina," *Panorama Económico.* Santiago, Chile, November–December 1959.

Economic Commission for Africa, *The Significance of Recent Common Market Developments in Latin America,* Doc. E/CN.14/64. Addis Ababa, December, 1960.

Economic Commission for Latin America (ECLA), *Consultations on Trade Policy. Report of the Third Series of Meetings, Between Colombia, Ecuador and Venezuela* (Quito, December 7 to 10, 1960). Doc. E/CN.12/555. Santiago, Chile, March 1961.

——, *Derechos aduaneros y otros gravámenes y restricciones a la importación en países latinoamericanos, y sus niveles promedios de incidencia.* Doc. E/CN.12/554. Santiago, Chile, February 1961.

——, *Economic Survey of Latin America 1956.* United Nations, 1957. Publ. No. 57. II. G. 1. Part Three: A. "Preliminary Study of the Effects of Postwar Industrialization on the Composition of Imports and External Vulnerability of Latin America."

——, *Influence of the Common Market on Latin American Economic Development.* Doc. E/CN.12/C.1/13. April 14, 1959. (See ECLA, *The Latin American Common Market,* Part B.)

——, *Inter-Latin American Trade: Current Problems.* United Nations, 1957. Publ. No. 57. II. G. 5.

——, *International Co-operation in a Latin American Development Policy.* United Nations, 1954. Publ. No. 54. II. G. 2.

——, *Report of the Ninth Session.* Doc. E/CN.12/573 Rev.

1. Santiago, Chile, May 1961 (United Nations, Economic and Social Council, Doc. E/3486.)

———, *Report of the Trade Committee on the First Meeting of the Working Group on Customs Matters.* Doc. E/CN.12/568. Santiago, Chile, March 1961.

———, *Study of Inter-Latin American Trade.* United Nations, 1956. Publ. No. 56. II. G. 3.

———, *Study of Inter-Latin American Trade and its Prospects: Southern Zone of Latin America.* United Nations, 1953. Publ. No. 53. II. G. 4.

———, *The Latin American Common Market.* United Nations, 1959. Publ. No. 59. II. G. 4.

———, *The Latin American Movement Towards Multilateral Economic Co-operation.* Doc. E/CN.12/567. Santiago, Chile, March 1961.

———, Trade Committee, *Consultations on Trade Policy. Summary Record of Meetings Held at the ECLA Headquarters.* Santiago, Chile, August 26 to September 1, 1958. Doc. E/CN.12/C.1/11.

———, Trade Committee, *Some Problems of the Latin American Regional Market.* Doc. E/CN.12/C.1/WG.2/2. Santiago, Chile, January 25, 1958.

ECLA/FAO, *The Role of Agricultural Products in a Regional Market.* E/CN.12/499. April 7, 1959.

———, *The Role of Agriculture in the Latin American Common Market and Free-Trade Area Arrangements.* Doc. E/CN.12/551. Santiago, Chile, January 1961.

Esteves, Vernon R. "Desarrollo del mercado común latinoamericano." *El Trimestre Económico,* Vol. XXVI, No. 103. Mexico, July–September 1959.

Federal Reserve Bank of New York, "The Emerging Common Markets of Latin America," *Monthly Review,* New York, September 1960.

Ferrero, Rómulo A. *El mercado común latinoamericano.* Cámara de Comercio de Lima. Lima, Perú, 1959.

García Reynoso, Plácido. "Dos conferencias sobre el mercado común latinoamericano," *El Trimestre Económico,* Vol. XXVI, No. 104. México, October–December 1959.

————, "Problemas de integración industrial latinoamericana," *Comercio Exterior*, México, October 1959.

Garrido Torres, José. "Por qué um mercado regional latino-americano?" *Revista Brasileira de Política Internacional*. 1st Year, No. 2. Río de Janeiro, Instituto Brasileiro de Relaçoes Internacionais, June 1958, pp. 74–121.

Gordon, Lincoln. "Economic Regionalism Reconsidered," *World Politics*, Vol. XIII, No. 2, Princeton, N.J., January 1961.

Gómez, Rodrigo. *Discurso del señor Rodrigo Gómez, Director General del Banco de México, S.A. ante la XXIV Convención de Banqueros de México*. Acapulco, April 1958. (See *Comercio Exterior*, México, April 1958, pp. 188–190.)

Márquez, Javier. *Posibilidad de bloques económicos en América Latina*. México, El Colegio de México, 1944. (*Jornadas*, No. 16.)

Massard, Carlos, and Strassman, John. "Coordinación de la política económica dentro de la zona latinoamericana de libre comercio," *Comercio Exterior*, México, April 1961.

Méndez, Jorge. "La zona latinoamericana de libre comercio: una grave responsabilidad colombiana," *La Nueva Economía*, Vol. I, No. 1. Bogotá, February 1961.

Méndez Delfino, Eustaquio. "La integración económica y el mercado común de Latinoamérica," *Anales de la Academia de Ciencias Económicas*, Vol. III, Series 3. Buenos Aires, 1959.

Mikesell, Raymond F. "The Movement Toward Regional Trading Groups in Latin America," in *Latin American Issues: Essays and Comments* (ed. by Albert O. Hirschman). New York, Twentieth Century Fund, 1961.

Organization of American States, Inter-American Economic and Social Council, *Liberalization of Inter-Latin American Trade*. Economic Research Series. Report prepared by Prof. Raymond F. Mikesell. Washington, D.C., Pan-American Union, 1959.

Pegurier, Augusto. "O mercado comun latino-americano," *Economica Brasileira*, Vol. IV, Nos. 3 and 4. Rio de Janeiro, 1958.

Pinto Santa Cruz, Aníbal. "Antecedentes y razón de ser de la integración económica regional," *Panorama Económico*. Santiago, Chile, February and March, 1960.

Plaza, Galo. "A Latin American Regional Market," *Foreign Affairs*, New York, July 1959.

Prebisch, Raúl. "El mercado común latinoamericano," *Comercio Exterior*, México, September, 1959.

——, "Joint Responsibilities for Latin American Progress," *Foreign Affairs*, New York, July 1961.

Stanford Research Institute, Industrial Development Center, *Common Markets and Free Trade Areas: Problems and Issues for the United States*. Menlo Park, Calif., January 1960.

Sumberg, Theodore A. "Free-Trade Zone in Latin America," *Inter-American Economic Affairs*, Vol. 14, No. 1. Washington, D.C., 1960.

United States Senate, Subcommittee on American Republics Affairs, Foreign Affairs Committee, *United States and Latin American Policies Affecting their Economic Relations*. Report Prepared by the National Planning Association. 86th Congress, 2d session. Washington, D.C., Government Printing Office, January 31, 1960.

Uri, Pierre. *Suggestions Concerning the Latin American Regional Market*. ECLA, Trade Committee, Santiago, Chile, January 20, 1958. Doc. E/CN.12/12/C.1/WG.2/3.

Urquidi, Víctor L. "Apreciación preliminar del proyecto de Montevideo," *Comercio Exterior*, México, October 1959.

——, "El mercado común y el desarrollo económico nacional," *Comercio Exterior*, México, November 1959.

——, "The Idea of the Latin American Common Market," *Economic and Statistics Review of Puerto Rico*. The Puerto Rico Economics and Statistics Association, San Juan, Puerto Rico. Vol. II, No. 1. First half, 1961.

——, "The Common Market as a Tool of Economic Development," in *Latin American Issues: Essays and Comments* (ed. by Albert O. Hirschman). New York, Twentieth Century Fund, 1961.

————, "The Montevideo Treaty: A Comment on Mr. Sumberg's Views," *Inter-American Economic Affairs*, Vol. 14, No. 2. Washington, D.C., 1960.

Urrutia Millán, Rafael. "Aspectos fiscales del tratado de la zona de libre comercio de Latinoamérica," *Comercio Exterior*. México, April 1960.

Vallejo, Joaquín. "Comentarios sobre el proyecto de mercado regional interlatinoamericano," *Ciencias Económicas*, Vol. V, No. 12. Medellín, Colombia, May 1958.

Wionczek, Miguel S. "El financiamiento de la integración económica de América Latina," *El Trimestre Económico*, Vol. XXVII, No. 105, January–March 1960.

————, "The Montevideo Treaty and Latin American Economic Integration," *Quarterly Review*, Banca Nazionale del Lavoro. Rome, No. 57, June 1961, pp. 197–240.

PAYMENTS COMPENSATION

Bello, Daniel J. "Los pagos y el mercado común regional," *Comercio Exterior*. México, November 1959.

Bueno, Gerardo. "La zona de libre comercio y el problema de pagos," *Comercio Exterior*. México, February 1960.

Central Bank of the Argentine Republic, "Régimen cambiario y de pagos argentino y su tendencia al multilateralismo," *Memoria [de la] V Reunión de Técnicos de los Bancos Centrales del Continente Americano*. Bogotá, Banco de la República, 1957. Vol. I, pp. 303–376.

Centro de Estudios Monetarios Latinoamericanos, *Aspectos monetarios de las economías latinoamericanas*. México, 1959. Chapter III-3.

Economic Commission for Latin America (ECLA), *Multilateral Compensation of International Payments in Latin America*. Santiago, Chile, May 1949. Doc. E/CN.12/87.

————, *Papers on Financial Problems Prepared by the Secretariat . . . for the Use of the Latin American Free-Trade Association*. Doc. E/CN.12/569. Santiago, Chile, March 1961. This document includes the following:

A. Payments and Credits in the Free-Trade Area Projected by Latin American Countries. Possible Systems.
B. Further Considerations on the System of Swing Credits in the Free-trade Area.
C. Report of the Meeting of Governmental Representatives of Central Banks to the Second Session of the Inter-Governmental Conference for the Establishment of a Free-Trade Area among Latin American Countries.
D. The Reciprocal Credits System for the Free-trade Area.

Portnoy, Leopoldo. "El sistema multilateral de comercio y pagos, París Club," *Revista de Ciencias Económicas*, Series IV, No. 46. Buenos Aires, January–March 1958.

Prebisch, Raúl, "Los pagos multilaterales en una política de mercado común latinoamericano," in *Suplemento al Boletín Quincenal*, México, Centro de Estudios Monetarios Latinoamericanos, December 1958, pp. 274–283. (Statement to the Second Meeting of the Working Group of Central Banks, ECLA, Rio de Janeiro, November 24, 1958.) Also published in *Revista del Banco de la República Oriental del Uruguay*, 17th Year, No. 68. Montevideo, January 1959.

Swenson, Louis N. "El intercambio y los pagos regionales en la América Latina," *Memoria [de la] V Reunión de Técnicos de los Bancos Centrales del Continente Americano*. Bogotá, Banco de la República, 1957. Vol. V, pp. 197–211.

Triffin, Robert. *Europe and the Money Muddle: from Bilateralism to Near-Convertibility*. New Haven, Yale University Press, 1957.

————, "La América Latina en el comercio y en los pagos mundiales," *Memoria [de la] V Reunión de Técnicos de los Bancos Centrales del Continente Americano*. Bogotá, Banco de la República, 1957. Vol. V, pp. 119–142.

————, *Possibility of Effecting Multilateral Compensation Settlements between Latin American and European Countries through the European Payments Agreement.* ECLA, Santiago, Chile, March 4, 1953. Doc. E/CN.12/299.

Villaseñor, Eduardo. "The Inter-American Bank: Prospects and Dangers," *Foreign Affairs,* New York, October 1941.

CENTRAL AMERICA

Economic Commission for Latin America (ECLA), *Análisis y perspectivas del comercio intercentroamericano, 1934–38 a 1946–52.* Doc. E/CN.12/367, July 20, 1955.

———, "Central American Economic Integration Programme: Evaluation and Prospects," *Economic Bulletin for Latin America,* Vol. IV, No. 2. Santiago, Chile, October 1959.

———, *La integración económica de América Central: su evolución y perspectivas.* United Nations, 1956. Publ. No. II. G. 4.

———, *Política comercial y libre comercio en Centroamérica.* Doc. E/CN.12/368, July 20, 1955.

———, Central American Economic Cooperation Committee, *Report of . . . September 3, 1959 to December 13, 1960.* Doc. E/CN.12/552. United Nations, 1961. Publ. No. 60. II. G. 7.

El Salvador, Ministry of Economy. *El programa de integración económica de Centroamérica.* San Salvador, 1958.

Organization of Central American States. *Integración económica de Centroamérica.* First Seminar on Central American Economic Integration. Vol. I. (San Salvador, Secretariat of the Organization of Central American States, 1959.)

Sol, Jorge. "La integración económica de Centroamérica y los programas nacionales de desarrollo económico," in *Integración económica de Centroamérica.* Vol. I. Organization of Central American States. San Salvador, 1959, pp. 37–71.